Welcome!

Canada Diary
Chasing The Simple Life

by Natalie Bruckner

FOR MY FAMILY, MY ARMY

AND SO IT BEGINS....It started with a dream; a dream to live the simple life. To wave goodbye to the rat race of the UK and go back to nature. Ten years ago, in pursuit of this dream, Natalie and Nathan waved goodbye to their family and friends and headed to Vancouver, British Columbia in Canada.

This is a heartfelt, raw, comical, and yet sometimes heartbreaking biographical story of the struggles faced by what many considered to be the "perfect couple" of moving to a new country, how their dreams came to fruition, and eventually tore them apart. Dreams change, but Canada will always be their home.

***

PROLOGUE

Many of us at some point in our lives think, "Is this all there is?"

There must be more to life than working 9am to 5pm, or more likely, 8am to 6pm? More to life than this rat race. The simple life is calling. In fact it's shouting my name.

Imagine going from a fast-paced materialistic lifestyle where the car you drive and the postal code you live in defines who you are and turning up in a new land with nothing aside from a dream; a dream that will ultimately help you understand what's really important in life.

For many immigrants, Canada represents this dream. A land full of opportunities, a land so rich with nature, so open-minded . . . a place that offers more than just *work work work* and earning just enough to go on vacation for a few weeks a year. Dreaming and planning all year for that one or, maybe two weeks of vacation. There has to be more to life, and that can be found in Canada. Can't it?

Mountains. Lakes. Nature! Living life as it should be lived. Back to basics as they say.

But, let's be honest, nothing is quite that black and white. I wrote this story to bring you an honest look at the realities behind my own experience of chasing a dream to a new land: the challenges of moving to Canada (from understanding the housing market to healthcare and relationship pressures); the opportunities that living in Canada presents; the highs and the lows; and ultimately, to lead us to the BIG question…"What are you really willing to give up to live that dream?"

Nathan and Natalie arrive in Canada with nothing aside from what they can carry in their suitcases and a ship load of CDs and vinyl, and yet over the next 10 years Canada provides them with opportunities to build a mini empire: becoming landlords; running businesses; and ultimately losing something they never thought they would lose.

***

CONTENTS

LIFE HAS SO MANY CHAPTERS...AND SO DO I!

***

Chapter 1

ON THE MOVE
(November 2007)

We've finally done it.

We're on the plane ready to start our new life in Canada. OH MY GOSH . . we are actually starting a new life in Canada, eh!

Emigrating is one of those things that people talk about, but few people I know actually end up doing for one reason or another – but here we are, boxes shipped, bags packed, farewells completed and we are ready to start all over again. A.G.A.I.N! Gosh, I feel like Christopher Columbus, only I haven't discovered new land, I am not travelling by sea, and I definitely don't have one of those weird looking sailor's hats. Not yet anyway, let's see what the fashion is in Canada.

Before I get too carried away, let me introduce myself. My name is Natalie Bruckner and I am a 32-year-old journalist. The name is quite a mouthful I know, but when I married Nathan I wasn't willing to give up what I considered was my "identity."

You see I had fought for what the name Bruckner stood for. As you can probably tell by the name, I am of German descent. I know, I know, before you come up with your smart quips, I do have a sense of humour (at least I think I do) and I don't reserve sunbeds by the swimming pool. Now, where's my towel?

Growing up I had been called Hitler so many times I actually started to think that was my name. Defending the Bruckner surname and what it stood for had become, well, a part of me. I was fortunate enough to have grown up hearing both the English and German experiences of war (don't mention the war, I jest of course, thanks Fawlty Towers for that one). What our grandparents generation lived through – and were sheltered from – is something that made them into the amazingly strong people they are/were and their stories are something we can only hope to learn from. Although, looking at what is happening today, I am not so sure about that.

Anyway, history/politics to one side for a second, I decided that a double-barreled German/Italian name just sounded, well, hilarious, and I will do almost anything for a laugh...I said almost, don't get carried away now.

Hindsight is indeed a wonderful thing. Had I actually thought about it and realized that every time I had to give my surname over the phone it would take me at least 10 minutes as I would have to say "yes, it's Bruckner-Menkeli....that's B.R.U.C.K.N.E.R. with an umlaut over the U, and then, hyphen, M.E.N.K.E.L.I, that's right M for, well muppet, E for eeejit..." you get the gist. Heaven forbid I had someone on the end of the line where there was a delay and whose first language wasn't English. We could be there for hours.

OK, so where was I? Oh yes, so we are on the plane, and in the seat beside me is my wonderful husband Nathan.

The story of how we met is like the plot from one of those wonderfully trashy girl's novels. You know the kind where girl meets boy when she was with her boyfriend while on a ski holiday, holiday is wonderful, but boyfriend likes his bevvies and ignores her. Six years later, after the girl has finally picked up the courage to end the relationship that has far exceeded its course, she bumps into the man of her dreams in a club and licks his face because she has had one too many barley pops (that's normal right)? The timing is all wrong, so the girl decides she doesn't want a relationship right now, the boy is persistent and hey ho, happily ever after.

Well, that would be that novel's version anyway.

Nathan was actually a friend of my ex-boyfriend's best friend's brother. Confusing? Yes. Awkward? Very!

I was going on a snowboarding holiday to Cormayeur in Italy with my then boyfriend, his best friend, his best friend's brother and all of his friends.

As was the case when I went on holiday with my then boyfriend, I became virtually invisible to him and was replaced by the wonderful amber nectar (better known in the U.K. as the good old brewski), so I ended up making friends with Nathan, and we had a great laugh together. Nothing more, honest, I'm just not that kind of girl.

A few years later and what do you know, the boyfriend becomes the ex and I meet up with Nathan in a club in Bournemouth and he decides to pursue me and tell me he is taking me on a date whether I like it or not. And the rest, as they say, is history.

Nathan is my toyboy. He is a whopping two-and-a-half years my junior (thanks Adrian Mole for that one). We have had our ups and down, as any relationship does, but we've managed to come out the other end smirking (note the use of the term).

So here we are, six years later, on a plane in London, destination, Vancouver, Canada. It has taken us three years to get here. No, not Canada, that would be silly, but it has taken us three years to get our permanent residency.

After a bout of travelling four years earlier where I was tired of working ridiculously early shifts as the head of news and female element of a morning show for a local radio station, and saving every miserly penny (I even had a penny jar) to seek out snow and escape from the work-and-show attitude that was so prevalent in the UK (oh, your sofa is how old? Mine is brand new), Nathan mentioned one evening that he needed an escape. He had enough of the humdrum life and wanted something more.

You see Nathan's mother had passed away from Cancer (which I will explain later when you are ready for a sad and, seemingly all too common tale regarding the life of our generation and the Big C). He mentioned moving to Canada and I thought, why not? Afterall, we were mountain and nature people. There was snow, mountains, people lived in igloos (what? Isn't that what everyone thinks of Canada), and it was just a damned exciting prospect. So we made the decision to apply for Canadian immigration. Also, my mum and dad had lived in Algonquin Park in Ontario during their early 20s and I had grown up watching slide after slide of images of bears, lakes, and mountains. Life was obviously ideal in Canada. (I blame you parents, lol).

Had we been called in for an interview by Citizenship and Immigration Canada and the what I consider to be scary immigration people had actually asked us why we wanted to move, I would have spoken in the best Queen's English and said that it is "because your economy is strong, the country provides plenty of opportunities for the younger generation, and has a forward-thinking attitude." While all these points are indeed true, the real reason was that we wanted to live somewhere with mountains and snow where we could snowboard every day. Thankfully I never did get called in for that interview.

Once we found out I had enough points under the Skilled Worker visa to get into Canada we went through the entire process using an immigration lawyer, who, as it turned out, was awesome.

Admittedly, the process wasn't painless. It took us three years, and a lot can happen in three years.

During those "years in purgatory" as I like to call them, I worked in Spain as a journalist on an English and German magazine and newspaper, which was great fun for me; working on stories connected to the Russian Mafia, finding a boss in an uncompromising position with a girl he had fired that morning (she got her job back the next day incidentally, talented girl obviously), and walking into the office one evening to discover another boss, rosy cheeked, sat in front of magazine pages that needed to be proofed and sent to the printers that night . . . well that was definitely an experience. But for Nathan our time in Spain was less of a positive, fun, quirky experience, and more of a slap in the face. It was the first time he had been out of work since he left school and Nathan is a proud man of Italian origin. Need I say more?

Nathan has what is known as the gift of the gab – he can sell chopsticks to the Chinese, poutine to the French Canadians, wurst to the Germans (you get what I am saying), but for once he was finding it impossible to get a job. It didn't help that he couldn't speak the language, and didn't have a knack for languages, and again, hindsight….. but we were young and the world was our oyster, right? So what I saw as an adventure, Nathan saw as his world coming crashing down around him. I should have seen it coming.

I got together with Nathan just after his mum had passed away. It was a terrible time for him, as you can imagine. He was 24 and I came along as a welcome distraction – not always a good thing when someone should be grieving. The honeymoon period of a new relationship during a time like this can only last so long before your past comes to bite you on the ass.

Looking back now I realize Nathan, like many of us, tried to run away from his problems – funny how they catch up with you eventually. You can run, but you can't hide – and I wasn't helping because, being someone who revels in adventures and a people-pleaser to boot, no sooner did he say "let's go here" or "let's do this" and my bags were packed and waiting by the door. Life is an adventure right, and you better enjoy the ride you were given.

This happened a few times. The first was in 2003 when we spent six months snowboarding in Breckenridge, Colorado. I was freelancing for a Denver paper and some sports magazines. Pretty much a dream for a newbie hack with a penchant for sports really. We are both snowboarders with snow for hearts and so living in a place where it would dump with snow every night (or "puke" as they called it in Breckenridge) and every morning be treated to the bluest of skies and the most pristine powder known to man was, well, paradise.

However, instead of loving every minute of this new-found freedom, the dark cloud of his mum's passing followed Nathan from the UK to the US. What do they say the three stages of grief are? First comes the shock and denial, then comes pain and guilt, and then, as if you haven't been through enough already, comes anger, frustration, and bitterness. I think Nathan was hit with them all at once. And, as is often the case, you take it out on your nearest and dearest.

When he wasn't on the mountain snowboarding he was telling me: he couldn't be with me any longer in case he ended up loving me too much and I died and he couldn't handle that; getting angry with anyone who still had a mother, and at times getting into fist fights because of it; and to put it politely, being a complete knob.

I can't even imagine what it must be like to lose the heart and soul of a family, but I'm only human and you can only put on a smile and be a punchbag for so long before the cracks start to show.

Needless to say, we had our spats. I remember the night clearly when I threw my engagement ring in the snow after experiencing an awful Christmas where I was shown just how death can make even the most wonderful man into a bitter and twisted anger machine . . .but we got through it. Little did I know, this was actually the calm before the storm.

Back to our time in Spain, which was in 2005, and Nathan had a breakdown. He saw the move as one of the worst experiences of his life – looking back he admits it was a wakeup call. It was time to either let life beat you down, or to wade through one of life's shit storms with your wellies on and then spray them off the other side. Spain obviously wasn't working, despite the support of my amazing mum and dad who lived there, so it was time to go back to Bournemouth, England (le sigh) and see if we could actually pressure wash him down.

As it happened, that minor breakdown gave me back the Nathan I had fallen head over heels with. My sister, by chance, had come across an article in one of her magazines that raised questions regarding depression. She gave it to Nathan who actually took it graciously and figured, that yes, he answered yes to nine out of the 10 questions on "Are you suffering from depression," and off he went the next week to the doctor. Kudos to him for that, that's for sure. It's a hard thing to admit.

I can't say I am pro-Prozac (or any kind of prescription drug for that matter), but a short stint for Nathan put him back on track – I say short because he stayed on them for two months, and despite doctor's orders he just stopped them one day, suffered a few harrowing days as a result, but came out the other end smiling. Btw, not recommended people. As they say on those ads, please consult a physician.

For Nathan, this did the trick, however. He was ready to tackle whatever life had to throw at him again, and that meant the itchy feet were back . . . no not athlete's foot, I mean the wanderlust, and yes, my bags were packed and by the door again ready to head across the Atlantic. Ooh another adventure.

Did we know much about Canada? Well I wouldn't say we thought everyone was a lumberjack and they were OK, that they worked all night and slept all day (such a classic skit that, thanks Monty Python), but we had only visited Canada on a couple of occasions, and only ever visited Vancouver once.

But we had made up our minds. Vancouver was to be our new home. It was close to the mountains, very close in fact with the local North Shore mountains just 20 minutes drive from downtown, and it was a big city, so jobs would be easier to come by. We had told everyone now, there was no turning back, and it just somehow felt right, you know? If I say I will do something, I will do it, even if I cut off my nose to spite my face (yes, yes mum, I know. But who do I take after, hmmm?). But I always weigh up the risks, get advice from those I trust, and then make up my own mind and go with my gut.

So three months after starting the process, copious amounts of paperwork, one wedding (that was us, we decided to get married in Bermuda midway through the process in 2005 and so we had to prove Nathan wasn't using me for a green card as we were getting in on me being the skilled worker. This consisted of all our personal letters to each other, letters from friends to say how we had met, documents proving vacations away. saucy photos, (oh no wait, but jeez, it may have well have been...what a hassle) and we finally got the yes. Thank-goodness. We'd been going out of our minds in the UK.

The first year of waiting to hear if we were eligible for the Skilled Worker visa was fine, we didn't expect to hear anything. I was working as a journalist for a local newspaper, which was great. I was editing a prestigious magazine that gave me a chance to interview the likes of Joan Collins, Nigel Mansell, and Richard Attenborough, and I was allowed to come up with article ideas such as, "Should you buy a Ferrari or a helicopter?" I got to go out and test the theory. By the way, the helicopter won purely because of the dismal traffic in the UK.

It's fair to say my work/life definitely did not suck.

The second year we started to get anxious. Our lives were on hold. We'd moved from one property to the next and finally settled in an area we fondly called Bos-scumb on the edge of crime central. In truth, Boscombe wasn't all that bad, in fact it was a pretty cool location, close to the beach and Bournemouth town centre. This is where my father-in-law bought a flat for us to rent – I think secretly hoping we would decide against the move and settle down to have a family (well, he is Italian and looks like a cross between Al Pacino and Robert De Nero). It was the first time I felt kind of at home since moving out of our family home in Southbourne.

The third year was just plain tiresome if I'm honest. We had started to give up hope. We didn't hear anything back from immigration, not a dicky bird, and despite a stack of paperwork the height of a three-storey building, we thought we might have missed some essential elements to the process. I was working for pretty low pay (the life of a journalist) and all anyone ever seemed to do when we went to social gatherings was judge us for not owning a property yet, and being perhaps what they would consider whimsical. I'm sure they didn't really, and we were just projecting, and even if they did, I get it, I do. We were in our 30s and we had been talking about this for three years and nothing, absolutely nothing, had changed.

Nathan had already given up. But just when I was fighting with every breath to stay positive, and drawing some rather raspy ones, we got an email from the law firm to say we'd been given an interview waiver and we were in.

We were off to Canada: O Canada! Our home and native land!

***

Chapter 2

SAYING GOODBYE
(November 2007)

OK, so if I could learn from my mistakes I would pack A LOT sooner, say my goodbyes to everyone A LOT earlier, and not have spent all that money on boots and shoes, because they really don't pack very well.

We had originally decided to move to Vancouver the following April (2008); and that gave us just under one year. Plenty of time to get everything sorted, right? Too much time it seemed.

Somehow we both came up with the bright idea late one evening (when all the best ideas happen) that we should move the date forward so we could be snowboard instructors for the season, you know, take time out of our careers before finding what we call "real jobs." Sorry instructors, but as you know, while it can be a really tough job at times, the pay just sucks and you do it for love (unless you are willing to head up through the ranks), and we wanted to buy a house and establish our roots in the only way we knew how. The true British way I suppose. Moving for the winter season would also allow us to make friends with like-minded people (we were leaving behind such an amazing group of mates) and we could make contacts while we were instructing.

So we suddenly went from moving in one year to moving in seven weeks! Gulp.

Fortunately, somehow everything seemed to fit into place. They say that when you've chosen the right path, you know, and if I wasn't mistaken we had climbed onboard the express train, destination Canada.

The first major hurdle was telling the editor of the publishing house I was working for that I would be leaving, and soon, in fact very soon.

You see the thing is, I had worked at the local newspaper for a very, very long time. I started as a rookie, working for six years as a journalist and features writer, had proudly won a few awards (which is always nice), featured on radio and become fairly well-known in a Z-rate celebrity style status (you know, I even got recognised by a 82-year old granny in a supermarket and had some guy in a club recognize my voice and tell me he had recorded every show I had been on, creepy . . . yea Chris Evans, eat your heart out). In all honesty I was getting bored and recognition for working like a nutter isn't really a "thing" in the UK from my experience..."oh, you are good at that job and you aren't constantly whining about pay? Well, let's just milk you a little more."

I'd become a bit too comfortable and was getting a little tired of earning just enough to get by, as many fellow journalists will understand.

My career at the newspaper was followed by a paddle in the radio river as I mentioned. I joined the local radio station as head of news and as the female element of the morning crew.

My short career of just under a year there was fun, nuts, and an absolute mind-mess because of the early morning starts. It seems getting up ay 5am in the winter isn't my thing. Also, I'm pretty sure my mates thought I was a one trick pony as the only stories I had when I met up with them were the same ones they had heard me tell on the radio that morning. I was boring. I was overtired. My brain was a fog.

So I was done with mixing a bubbly "good morning everyone, what a great day" personality (with the help of copious amounts of energy drinks) with a hard news nose where I would have to call the police voice bank each and every morning and hear about stabbings and people being glassed at the nightclub central that Bournemouth had become. . . what was happening to the world? It was doing my rose-tinted glasses persona no good. No good at all. It can be hard to see the light when you are constantly rummaging in the dark.

That's when the opportunity to go to Colorado came along. A chance to step into a Sound Of Music style lifestyle.

So where was I? Oh yes, newspaper, me handing my notice into my editor so I could head off to Canada. I had returned from our travels (Colorado and Spain) and joined the newspaper again. The editor was such a lovely man and he welcomed me back with open arms after returning from Spain. So, telling my editor (who was more of a friend), that I was off again was really, really tough.

I say told him . . . that's if you can count writing two resignations, the official one and the other explaining why I was off so early, as *telling* him. Yes, I'm a coward. I just thought if he read why first it would make things easier. And it did.

I walked into his office on Monday morning and he smiled at me. Oh my God! Was he pleased to see me go? Had he not read the letter? What would I say?

As it happened, he'd read them both and said it was the kind of dream he would love to fulfill. After telling me to, in his words, "bugger off b****" we hugged and spoke about my future plans of owning a chalet in the mountains with two golden retrievers (or, if Nathan had his way, two Springer Spaniels). My editor's eyes lit up as he told me I was pursuing his dream, of how he wanted to leave the country and live a simple life. As life so often turns out, he actually managed to follow his dream for a while before he was taken by the Big C a few years later at the age of 54. One of life's true legends taken far too early, that's for certain. He touched every life he ever came across.

Suddenly moving had become very real. Numerous farewell parties later and the time had come. We'd saved enough for a deposit on a nice house in the Okanagan Valley of B.C.'s Interior, well, have you seen the prices of Vancouver? We'd attempted to open a bank account with HSBC who had a branch or some kind of affiliation with a bank in Canada, but we were too late as they informed us you needed to have an account with them for a while before you can look into opening one in Canada – so we ended up going with a money exchange company, which turned out to be the best move for us.

(Sidenote: HSBC and other banks now actually do have an international link, as long as you set up an account 30 days or more before. Definitely worth checking long before you go, or, indeed, check out reputable money exchange companies.)

We'd reserved a bank account with TD Canada Trust bank while we were still in the UK so it could be ready for our money transfer (oh please, please, please don't let anything go wrong) and we'd even managed to meet with a friend of a friend called Hank (classic North American name) who was moving back to Vancouver, had hired a shipping container and said we could throw our belongings in with his. Another sign perhaps? Sad to say, our whole life managed to fit into my VW Golf.

The worst bit about all of this for me was leaving my sister behind. We're like Siamese twins, only not physically joined and we don't really look like each other (although we are starting to more and more as we get older, go figure). But she'd got herself a good man called Ben, who incidentally looks a bit like a Royal family member (I still think there has to be some connection). He is the real true English gentleman, but with a fantastically wicked streak. Plus my sister worked as cabin crew for an airline, so had more chance than anyone to come over and see us. That's a plus, right? I have to find the positives. OMG, I was going to miss her.

For Nathan, the hardest part was leaving his dad. His dad reminds me of a 1930s gentleman, with all the morals and manners to match, but is also of a generation that believes a woman's place is in the home cooking, ironing, cleaning and popping out babies, and I am the last person on earth like that. But somehow we had formed an absolutely amazing relationship. He accepted my "new" ways, and I appreciated his old-school style and honesty. He has a good heart, and while I will never be able to see things clearly through his lens, he was always very kind to me.

Anyway, as it seems is the case with a lot of men whose partners have passed away, he rather quickly found himself a lady who could fill the empty hole that the mother and heart of the family had left when she was sadly taken. He is very open and admits he can't be alone, cook for himself, or do all the household chores. After being with Nathan for just a week I remember him asking me "don't you do Nathan's ironing?" It's a generational thing (she says, swinging the iron by the chord and throwing it into the nearest wall); although my dad is quite the opposite of that and what many may refer to as a new age man.

My father-in-law, however, has mellowed lots over the years. He has had to, the poor man. I'm the sort of woman who believes there's nothing wrong with a househusband. Well, like I said, I grew up with my father, who, if you don't mind me showboating for a second, is a top chef who has cooked for the Queen, Krushchev, The Beatles and Lorne Green, you know that guy off Bonanza? He thinks nothing of cooking and cleaning, and my mum worked long hours as she was extremely career driven later in life, before she would come home to do the ironing, as she considered that her thing. I think it's now called a "pink job" rather than a "blue job," or something like that. And so the classic gender roles didn't really exist in my world growing up. It was a case of pitching in where you can, and love and family always came first.

So yes, leaving family is hard. I won't sugar coat that. It sucks. Utterly sucks.

After a teary goodbye at the airport (don't ever do that, it's the worst thing to do), we had made it. So far so good. The next hurdle would be questioning at immigration, which I'd heard would be SS style, oh joy.

***

Chapter 3

CREW, GET READY FOR LANDING
(November 2007 – the next day)

Ten hours later, on a very packed flight, we finally landed, in all senses of the word. Nathan had gone deathly silent. He had what I call his slapped arse face on. When he gets worried or stressed he tends to get this angry look, he goes quiet, and dare I say anything he will snap "No" whether I'm right or wrong.

I've learned to be quiet in these times. We all handle stress differently. You know those women who've been with their husbands for so long all they do is roll their eyes when their husbands do something. Yes, that was me already.

To be fair, he had a very good reason to be worried. We could get turned back. Going through immigration isn't easy, even when you're just a visitor. You don't have to be wearing a ticking rucksack to get the Spanish inquisition. How do they somehow make you feel you have done something wrong, even when you're a law-abiding citizen?

Also, as chance would have it, for the first time ever, well the first time I'd ever heard of, the newspapers in Canada had reported numerous incidents where people had been tasered, and died. That's right, tasered . . . and died. Just a few weeks before one guy had been moving to Canada and had been zapped, and yes, had died. The actual details were yet to be released, so who knows what went on, but not something you really want to read.

So if I'm being a drama queen, to me this could actually be a life and death situation. Now was not a time to start with the dry English sense of humour. The queue was massive. The faces on the immigration officers were enough to make anyone poop their pants. Oh joy. One guy in particular was being particularly ruthless to a guy in front of us. I just hoped we didn't get him.

Guess what. We did! Yay.

We approached with nervous smiles. All of a sudden the man's attitude changed, he asked us a few questions to make sure we had enough funds to cover ourselves and said "Welcome to Canada-eh," with a big smile. Fabulous. What a sweetheart. It's obviously all about your attitude.

The only hurdle now was that you don't receive your permanent resident's card for eight weeks until after you've landed, and that's after you've secured a permanent address, which we still didn't have, as we had no idea about the areas yet. The thing is you see, until you get your permanent residency card, you can't leave the country because you have to go through the whole visa application process again.

Why would we want to leave the country anyway, you may ask? Well, we don't really, aside from the fact my sister was getting married in Austria in February, and with Christmas coming up, I started to panic that this could be a little close. I wouldn't miss my sister's wedding, no matter what. No, no, no, positive thinking, don't panic yet, I'm sure the PR card will arrive in time . . . once we've found a place to live that is.

We grabbed our bags, consisting of the heaviest suitcases known to man and two snowboard bags that even Nathan Tyson would have had difficulty lugging around, and we limped out of the airport like the Hunchback of Notre Dame to the taxi rank. The bells, the bells!

What on earth is that bright light in the sky?

The sun! That's a first. I'd heard Canada rains non-stop during the winter. Or that's what my brother-in-law-to-be kept saying to wind me up, and all those people who would respond with a, "why do you want to move to Canada, it's so cold."

We got into the cab, driven by this lovely East Indian guy who'd immigrated to Vancouver 20 years ago to the day. That will be us one day.

***

Chapter 4

BFFS

We'd tried to get as prepared as possible so nothing would shock us when we emigrated.

There's kind of an unspoken rule amongst the British that when you tell them you're emigrating they say, "oh, how nice" but behind that smile they're thinking "you'll be back." (Admit it, you read that bit with an Arnold Schwarzenegger accent didn't you?)

Come on now, what is it with us Brits? Not only have we often lost the ability to appreciate one another at work, and so often, sadly, at home and in society in general, but should anyone try to follow a dream, there's always a sense of cynicism attached.

We have our dry wit, that's for sure, but there's this will for, what is it? Failure? Just look at the British press whenever there's a World Cup on or some other big sporting event. We begin slating our own, even before they've set foot on the pitch.

I know some friends didn't, and perhaps still don't think I will stay in Canada, and although as my mother used to say, never say never, I now know that I will never move from Canada. It has my heart. Its optimism, opportunities, outdoor/nature, its people – it changes you. But anyway, digression, more about that later.

In order to make sure we didn't fail at our move, we had done our research. We'd watched the property market and the economy for the past three years. The Vancouver Sun newspaper and The Globe and Mail alternated as our homepage and we'd signed up to every newsletter on moving to Canada or the job and property market that was in existence. The most useful of which turned out to be a website called relocation2bc, which was set up by an English couple who'd moved to Vancouver 20 years ago (and is actually still in existence, but dormant).

Despite this, and a million other sites, we were unable to find a short-term rental. It seems everyone and his brother knows someone who lives in

Vancouver, and yet not one of them knew of somewhere that would do a short-term let. And we wanted short-term as we needed to figure out the different areas before we started to lay serious roots.

So after saying "no thanks" to numerous one-year rentals in people's basements – which, incidentally, is the norm in Vancouver and is actually a lot more luxurious and spacious than many of our flats in England – we weren't being picky, we just wanted somewhere we could feel safe.

Yes, we were, I suppose, homeless? It wasn't that bad however as we did have a friend who was willing to put us up for a few days while we went in search of a flat, or what Canadians call a suite or an apartment.

I say friend, well Vicky, bless her heart, is now indeed a friend, but we had only met once before back in the 2003. Poor girl! We'd actually met through work in the UK She was working in PR for a major supermarket and we had got together over coffee in Salisbury, Wiltshire, as she was after some promotion for a new brand of shampoo for some famous stylist, and we just hit it off. You know that moment when you just click with someone?

I wasn't exactly the most trusting of people when it came to what I call "true friends." I had plenty of friends; great people who I can have a laugh and a drink with, but true friends, those who you can tell everything to and you know it won't go any further, someone that you can rely on 100 percent and who would be there for you when things go wrong, well they are hard to come by. I, like many girls, had a little bit of a rough experience as a kid. I mean now you look back and laugh, but as a little girl, it can seem like the end of the world and can really shape your future friendships.

It seems while boys often suffer from physical bullying, when it comes to emotional bullying, girls have that sh*t fine-tuned. I had a friend in school who I had known from a very young age. Like most little girls, my best friend would often swap from one-minute to the next, but when we hit secondary school and started to form stronger bonds, things became a little more challenging.

One friend liked to play mind games, but I didn't know any different. I mean, who teaches you that? Or does it come naturally for some women? Poor guys! This friend would hide from me with our other friends when I came round, or just make me feel like I wasn't a good enough friend and that I would be replaced if I didn't do as requested.

Silly things really, but when you're 11 and can't flick them the bird, get in your car and drive away, it's a pretty harsh lesson to learn early on. It wasn't an isolated incident either. I was shy as a kid and a bit of a pushover, which isn't good in the girl animal kingdom. So as you can imagine, my vision of friends was slightly distorted because no matter how trivial it seems now, that stuck like glue, dammit. I can see you girls nodding your heads. You've been there too, right? Girls can be vicious little things at school.

Well, I say I had trust issues with friends, that is until I met my best friend, bestie, bff, whatever you want to call her. Cath is her name. We met during an art class. We were both fairly quiet back then . . oh how things have changed. She was experiencing a similar sort of friendship, and so when we started talking and we realized, you know what, sod this, or sod them, or whatever you think at 12 (poop to you?), and we started hanging out together.

We just seemed to come out of our shells. We'd get constantly told off in class for talking too much, our so called former friends got a little funny with our friendship, and we didn't care (tables were turning, life lessons were being had) and we started building a very strong bond. Today Cath is my sister from another mister.

Honestly, Cath and I have so many secrets of all the shenanigans we have got up to that if we were to write them down, our book would rival the size of The Lord of The Rings.

We were sweet kids, honest mum, but when we look back now, we were naughty little devils too. That kind of bond is hard to find. From all this however I had learned to be a little more selective with my friends. I love people, don't get me wrong, they are interesting, fascinating, and for the most part, really good souls, but friends will always say that I have a glint in my eye that tells them when I've finally let them in.

I think I've just seen it happen too many times before. People who get too close too quick. It so often ends in tears. Saying this, ironically, when I met Vicky (my Vancouver friend) in a café in Salisbury, we just hit it off. Then we got onto the subject of Canada, don't ask me how (looking back, maybe I was obsessed and talking about it all the time), and it turned out Vicky and her boyfriend were emigrating to, yes you've guessed it, Vancouver.

Chance? Coincidence? Aligning stars? Or just one of the thousands of people immigrating every year, who knows?

So we kept in touch. Vicky however moved a few months after we first met. She had one distinct advantage to many of us; she was Canadian! She was born in Toronto, but had moved to the UK when she was eight.

Anyway, we kept in touch, and I was updated every now and then as to her progress. She had a job, a dog and bought an apartment. Super inspiring. I meanwhile was in the same job, same apartment, and getting a little frustrated, but she kept up the positive vibes from across the ocean.

Every time she would ask if we had heard anything, the answer was always the same. It became painful. I don't mean for me, but I could almost feel the dubiousness with how she approached the question.

She wasn't alone either. For two years after we had applied friends in the UK would ask us if we had heard anything, although it would become less frequent, and when they did, you could hear their voices quieten as they thought "should I ask now?"

So when we did get the yes, their eyes sparkled...no longer would they have to endure the torture of feeling like they had to ask, and wishing that their friends that just kept going on and on and on about moving to Canada would finally get their wish and bugger off so they'd have somewhere great to visit.

Where was I? Oh yes, back to Vicky, my Canadian friend. After countless dead ends when it came to the possibility of renting short-term, I asked her if she knew of anyone that needed some extra cash on the run-up to Christmas in exchange for a room for a week.

I know what you're thinking, and no, I didn't ask on the off-chance that she'd say, "come and stay with us." Seriously, no. The poor girl. I'd only met her once and for all she knew I could be the next cereal killer (yes granola, you're dead to me).

Despite this, she did offer. Bless her. I tried to decline saying that a guest is like a fish; if they stay for longer than three days they start to smell (credit to my German granny for that one, hey, hang on a second, maybe she'd been hinting all along...), but Vicky had insisted, and well, any help at this stage was welcome. Sometimes you just have to reach for the extended hand and push pride to one side. Afterall, people often only offer if they want to help, otherwise you will get radio silence from my experience.

So we were going to stay with a girl and her boyfriend who I'd only met once over a coffee in Salisbury.

"Hello? Natalie? WHAAA THE? OH MY God! OH MY God!"

OH MY God?

This was not quite the reception I'd expected when we arrived at Vicky's apartment in Vancouver. Oh no, was it all a joke? Had I been on Facebook messenger to someone else of the same name?

"Oh my God, what happened, I thought you guys were coming in tomorrow?" Oh thank goodness! That's all it was.

I could see the headline in the local papers: Brits Baited By Hoax Email. But instead we had somewhere warm to stay, which made our journey into the unknown that bit easier.

After an evening catching up on how Vicky's new life was going (both her and her boyfriend had found great jobs, settled themselves in and had a furkid), we hit the sack ready for our first full day in Canada.

The next morning it was time to get our Social Insurance Numbers (otherwise known as a SIN card). It's bizarre having to start again. In England you get your National Insurance card in your teens, and that's it, you tend to forget about it until you start a new job and ransack the house trying to find your card, or at least a payslip with the number on.

We felt like teenagers again.

So we decided to take the bus in the morning to the Sinclair Centre in Vancouver, where we would sign up for our SIN card *(note: you can now attend any Service Centre Canada office, which you can find on the Government of Canada website).* I had heard the process can be quite time-consuming, but after we found our way to the fourth floor, we waited seconds before we were called to the desk to explain what we were after.

We were then shown to another seat and were suddenly surrounded by Mexican construction workers. With the 2010 Winter Olympics coming up, Vancouver was crying out for anyone in the construction industry . . . why had I never thought about becoming a brickie?

Most people around us couldn't speak a word of English. If *we* felt daunted, I can't even imagine how you'd feel not being able to speak a word of English, oh apart from the word money, which everyone seems to know in this city as they approach you in clothes finer than those worn by the likes of Paris Hilton, especially down Robson Street.

Within a matter of minutes, we were called to a different desk, and, was I imagining this, or was this the same woman that was at the other desk? She read my mind, "Yes, I'm multi-tasking," she said, smiling.

A few forms later and we had our SIN numbers. Even though we didn't have an address yet. We were told we could just pick our cards up from the office two weeks later. That was simple. Next on the list? Time to pick up our health insurance forms, otherwise known as Medical Services Plan (MSP).

You see moving to Canada from England is great. They have a similar NHS system (only the payment doesn't come directly out of your wages, and instead you need to pay the MSP, every three months, so same same, but different), but you have to live in the province for 90 days before you're eligible. That meant we had to get ourselves covered by private insurance until MSP kicked in, but in order to apply we needed an address. Ah yes, fly, ointment. Oh well, we planned to get on the case this week.

Time for a coffee. In Canada, there's a Starbucks and Tim Hortons (Canada's national treasure and akin to Dunkin' Donuts in the US) on every street corner. Although the Canadians try to support their local businesses, after a visit to Tim Hortons, where the Cappuccino tastes like something your grandma used to make and the service was a fast-food, come-on-make-up-your-mind-I-want-to-get-you-out-of-here attitude, we make note to stick with Starbucks, or, Bean Around The World (great name and a Vancouver company. Yay. Go local).

Next stop, the seabus. I love the seabus. It takes you from downtown Vancouver to North Vancouver! We made the mistake of the paying the $2.25 bus fare one way and the $3.00 seabus fare separately and realized that for $8 you can buy a day pass that covers all the local transport *(as of 2019 this is now $10.25)*.

I say we discovered . . . it took quite some time. We visited the tourist information centre and were told we should buy a month pass which costs $58 (*sidenote: as of 2019 this is $95+*), but when we're directed to the newsagents where you can buy them, the kindly looking East Asian gentleman shook his finger at us and said, "No, not until later in the month. You buy special ticket now!"

So we scuttled off, and had to think about what we'd learned; 150 lashes for you, silly newbies.

Once on the seabus, we got a glorious view of the city and the mountains. I never realized North Vancouver, also known as the North Shore, was so big. To the west there are the more expensive homes in what is imaginatively called, wait for it, "West Vancouver" (which consists of the likes of Ambleside, Dundarave, and ironically, British Properties), to the East is Lynn Valley and Deep Cove, and in front lies a metropolis of a city known as North Vancouver.

What stands out when you compare downtown Vancouver to North Vancouver is that in the city the architecture is all glass, whereas the North Shore is very much New England style homes interspersed by the occasional Nelson Mandela tower and a growing number of glass curtain walled high-rises. Although that was about to change. It's such a city of contrasts.

At Lonsdale Quay in North Vancouver (the main strip), we pick up the North Shore News newspaper to look for apartments and head to another coffee shop where they are playing the acoustic version of Eric Clapton's Layla. Ah yes, that song will forever bring back memories of that moment.

We had left England with nothing. Furniture, crockery, everything was left with my father-in-law so he could rent out the apartment. Great in one way as we could start again, but that also meant we had to look for a furnished apartment and that's not the "done thing" it seems. That, and it's a lot more expensive to get a furnished place. Holyyyyyy, the North Shore is expensive.

Furnished places start at $1,600, which includes all utilities, compare that to an unfurnished townhouse in the suburbs and you're looking at saving $700 on that price. So we circled a few possibilities, which were in fact the only three places that were advertised as furnished, and we went to the corner store to buy a phonecard.

International phonecards here, we discover, are amazing. They give you hundreds of minutes for just $10. What we realized, after various expletives, was that you've still got to insert 25c to get through to the local number to be able to begin dialing. Note to self: Must keep quarters on me at all times, they are the staple food of the phone life diet when you don't have a mobile, or cell phone, in Canada.

I let Nathan do the talking, but I am doing the typical wife thing of standing by his side, telling him to not forget to mention we're married in case it helps. Oh lordy, when did I turn into this person?

We arrange our viewings for the next day and we decide to phone our families. I know that if I phone mine they won't be home. You see it's winter, so my parents are staying at their other villa in Spain, the one without the phone, so it's always a game of phone tag between us, which sucks for us both, but it is what it is.

It's quite sad in some ways because that, and the time zone differences, means I will rarely get to speak to them, as they only ever visit their house with a phone at lunchtime, which is 2am our time, when I am tucked up asleep!

So I leave a message on my mum's phone, picking out all the positives that have happened so far so they don't have to worry, because no matter how old you are, your parents will always worry. Then Nathan phones his dad, who is so pleased to hear from us, but also sounds on the verge of tears. Crikey, leaving people behind is hard.

Nathan's dad also tells us that his partner has decided to leave him, but says she's still in the house because she is unwell and he doesn't know what to do.

We get off the phone feeling quite, well, helpless . . . distance can be a bugger during these times, that's for sure. Then we get back on the seabus to head back to Vicky's. The city doesn't look quite so bright on the way back.

(Sidenote: You can actually apply online now for your MSP. However, as of February 22, 2018, to complete MSP enrollment adult Canadian Citizens and Permanent Residents need to obtain a Photo BC Services Card by visiting an Insurance Corporation of BC – ICBC – driver licensing office. There is no fee for the BC Services Card. You can

choose to combine it with your driver's licence, and fees that apply to the regular driver's licence application process apply.)

(Sidenote 2: Also, as of January 1, 2020 MSP premiums will be eliminated! Woohoo. No more phonecalls from MSP chasing me for outstanding payments.)

***

Chapter 5

SINS, BANKS, AND THE VANCOUVER
RENTAL DILEMMA
(Yup, Still November 2007)

It's day two in Canada and I wake up feeling super excited.

Today we are going to open up our bank accounts and go to see some potential new homes.

We grab a coffee and an $8 travel ticket. See, locals already! That was easy. Now it's time to get to grips with the bus timetable. There are so many buses, but the timetables don't seem to make sense. The weird thing is Vancouver isn't as big a city as you'd imagine. You can walk from one side to the other in a few hours, and there are so many landmarks, like Sears *(now Nordstrom)* and the Steam Clock in Gastown, that it's almost impossible to get lost, almost. But buses have a great knack of knocking your senses sideways, and as we discovered, you can end up quite confused on the wrong side of one of the many bridges. So many bridges.

After finding our way to Georgia and Granville Street (a main thoroughfare), we pop into Shoppers Drug Mart, a great place to buy your basics, including a much-needed hair dryer, mugs, spectacles, anything really, and then we are off to meet our new account manager at TD Canada Trust bank.

We walk in, and our account manager is stood at the counter. We introduce ourselves and she looks confused: "Oh I didn't realize it was today, it's not in the diary," she says. After various embarrassed looks from all parties, she checks the email we sent and confirms that yes, we have it right and that we must have been taken off the system. She fits us in anyway. Nathan has gone quiet. I don't think he is impressed.

As it turns out our account manager is an absolute gem. She arranges two bank accounts ready for our transfer. It's our first joint account. Ooh, I feel so grown up.

I've always avoided opening up joint accounts before. A case of cutting off my nose to spite my face really. I've always been so scared of being controlled when it comes to money that I've found every excuse in the book not to have one. Wise? Maybe. Only time will tell.

I can't imagine anything worse than working hard for your money and going out to treat yourself to a pair of running shoes, only to hear that voice in your subconscious that says "you'll be in real trouble lady."

But as we're in the same boat now, it does make a lot of sense.

After a successful bank meeting, where we sort out the accounts that would mean we aren't charged for taking money out at the ATM – or as Brits call it the cashpoint – as long as we keep a certain amount in the bank, and after getting some cheques, which apparently all Canadians use (yes there's no chip and pin here yet in 2007, and you still sign for things and use cheques), and we're off to the seabus again. Oh wait, did I mention you need to pay a monthly fee for most accounts in Canada? Well, that's something new for sure. I mean, it is minimal at around $30 a month, but still surprising coming from the UK.

We get to the North Shore and realize our calculations may be slightly out and that we've given ourselves hardly any time to get from one side of the city to the other to view apartments.

We manage to make it to the first appointment, we look at each other and just start laughing. "Is there any point in looking?" Nathan says. I decide it may be fun. What we're looking at is a concrete block containing 500 apartments – hardly what we envisioned for out idyllic wilderness Canadian dream!

We find the building manager, a strong set Hispanic lady who barks at us in a pleasant way, if there is such a thing. "If only people like you came sooner, we are all out. They've gone. All the apartments are taken. Possibly we have more coming up soon, come look, see what you think," she says. So we follow orders and walk down a dark corridor, head up in the elevator where you could imagine some horror movie being shot, and through to a one-bedroom apartment. The view from up here toward the mountain is absolutely stunning and the rooms are quite big, but it's just got this *feeling*. You just know exactly where you are, in a concrete block filled with people you'll probably never get to meet.

"You come and see a two bedroom, it's much bigger." Yes ma'am! So we follow our Hispanic friend to another corner of this dark block, and yes, she's right, it's much bigger, but it's still the same. For $1,400 a month I think we will have to decline her kind offer. Shame really because she ended up being quite a laugh.

I think she could tell from our faces that we would be running out the door, and after asking if we wanted to leave our details, and letting us use her phone to contact our next appointment (where in England would you get that?), she nods and wishes us adios.

Our next stop is at the other end of the North Shore and sounds quite promising. It's meant to be an old servants' house, but when we turn up outside the address, it's not quite as we imagined. It looks lovely, but it's all apartments and not a B&B as we read.

So we make a quick phonecall, or Nathan does anyway, and she says she's doing a viewing and to call in five minutes. Five minutes later we are outside and a woman shows us around the "servants' quarters."

The kitchen, the size of a shoe box, leads onto a bedroom, hardly big enough for a single bed, through to the lounge, which is currently being used as a bedroom because it's just about big enough.

I do all the necessary umms and ahhs, but can't wait to get out. Crikey, is this really what we can expect for $1,600 a month?

There's one place left to look at. It's just a short walk from where we are, so we call the building manager from a call box and arrange to meet.

As we walk along the road, we're surrounded by beautiful New England style homes, and well-cared for apartments where people say hello as you pass. The further on down the road we go, the more the scenery begins to change. We get to the apartment and opposite us are walls covered in graffiti, discarded shopping trolleys and people sat on their balconies smoking something that smells super, well, earthy. We walk in through the front door and the apartment looks promising. Inside there are wooden floors and the apartment itself is HUGE! It's a lot more than we hoped to spend at $1,800, but it does include bills and internet.

We are sorely tempted, until we are told that any guests that stay longer than seven days are considered tenants and you have to pay an additional $400 a month. As we've got two friends coming in a month for New Year with their little girl, this makes things quite difficult. We agree to get a two bedroom as we knew they would be coming, but we've already stretched ourselves.

We accept and tell the building manager we'll be back tomorrow afternoon with the deposit and first month's rent. That gives us time to mull it over.

***

After a great night out with Vicky and her boyfriend, and learning that no matter where you go in this great city you get the finest seafood for as little as $10, it's time to go apartment hunting, again.

We head across to the North Shore again early. Pick up that day's paper and realize there are no new rentals. A local sees us looking at the paper and says that rentals are so hard to come by in this town.

That's it. Sold. We're moving into the apartment we found yesterday, and we'll just have to warn our friends, or get around the extra guests clause somehow. We will figure it out. We had managed to wing it so far, so lets just see when the time comes.

After giving the building manager the deposit and signing the lease agreement, we walk away with the keys to the apartment and a small skip in our step. I say small because the price is worrying us a little, especially because we're not earning, and there are a few concerning clauses in the contract.

The next day Vicky and her boyfriend help us to move in, the little angels, and then leave us to get on with it. It feels so, well, alien. The flat is great, but we have no idea what this area is like, or what on earth the future holds. Exciting! Scary. Yikes.

We take a walk and I see a sign that says Squamish Nation land (this is quite ironic as you will later find out) and suddenly I'm filled with relief. Natives tend to have respect for their land and not material things and possessions, which would explain the graffiti. I'm so relieved, and quite exited. I've always found First Nation history fascinating. What amazes me even more is that when North Americans talk about their history they never seem to really include the Native history. Give me stories of elders, eagles, and rivers over Kings and Queens any day.

I get back to the apartment and log onto the internet and type in Squamish and find out that the Squamish Nation territory consists of 23 villages encompassing 28.28 square kilometers. These parcels of land are scattered from Vancouver to Gibson's Landing to the area north of Howe Sound. For some reason this makes me feel extremely contented.

We head off to the local lo-cost supermarket, which looked so close in the car but takes us more than 30 minutes to walk to (gosh I miss my car) and stock up on essentials consisting of butter, bread (which seems so expensive over here), vegetables, which are amazing value, and milk, which we can't quite figure out. There's one per cent, two per cent and three per cent, then there's no fat, skimmed, half

half, and about 10 different soya, almond and coconut milks. That's not including the goats milk and the milk in a bag (milkwutters). Time to experiment.

We decide it's also time to buy bedding as we don't have any. Now, here's the shock. A double bed is double here, but so is queen, and king is queen as we know it in the UK. Did I explain that well? Probably not, because it makes very little sense to me. Then the sheets have different measurements from single separate to king double and king separate! And there's the bed in a bag thing (Canada likes things in a bag it seems), an all-in-one bedding for your convenience. And the cost? Well duvet covers average around $100 from what we saw. Wilkinsons, where are you when I need you!

Even in Walmart the cost seems crazy. Bedding elsewhere, even on sale, comes to more than $300 plus tax, and the duvet covers are just so, well old-fashioned. You know the ugly floral ones your grandma used to have? The ones that are off-white and you're not sure if they are meant to be like that, stained by the sun, or something else? There's no neutral colours, just floral messes! Are we missing something? Do we just not know where to shop? Oh wait, yes, we've only just landed.

Patience . . . patience.

We opt for no duvet covers for now, and instead buy the bare essential, which of course consists of a soft throw, which turns out to be just a little bigger than a towel.

As we scratch our heads, I hear a couple from the north of England chatting. I walk up to them and it turns out they've lived here for 20 years and all the ex-pats meet once a month. We get invited along.

Now here's the thing. After working in Spain I've always had this thing about ex-pats just sticking with their own, but I decide it's stupid and realize these people have been in the same boat as we are now and are willing to help. So we swap emails and promise to meet in somewhere called the Dog and Hounds, or was it the Goose and Duck, or Bear and Cougar in a month.

(Sidenote: As of 2019, rentals are difficult to come by and the average cost of a one-bedroom in North Vancouver is around $2,000. The best places to look are craigslist, Facebook groups and by chatting with various experts at rental agencies.)

***

Chapter 6

SNOWBOARD INSTRUCTORS MAAAN,
SWEET

Time to meet our colleagues on the mountain! Yippee. Our new job will mean we will be meeting like-minded people and possibly new friends. It's so hard leaving old mates behind (who I feel will always be in our lives, no matter the distance), but I'm excited about meeting snow people! What will true Canadians be like? I sound like such a newbie!

It's day nine in Canada.

I feel like I've been here for a month and I'm
starting to get a bit despondent. I've sent off my CV
(resume over here) to about 10 magazines and
newspapers, and although it has only been two days
since I did that, I'm beginning to panic that maybe
media is as precious here as it was in the UK and
that all my years of experience will mean nothing.
Impatient much? I later realize that applying for just
10 jobs is ridiculous. Who did I think I was? Jon
Stewart?

Nathan on the other hand has got his first interview,
which is so amazing. He saw a job in the paper for a
car salesman for Ford and blitzed across his resume
(we better start speaking the lingo). The next
morning at 9am there's a phonecall for him while
he is in the shower. Guess what, they want to see
him. We are overjoyed, and freaking out!

We pop to Lonsdale Market to get some food, lug
that back to the apartment, which is four blocks
away but is painful as everything comes in big sizes
here, and then Nathan gets ready for his first
Canadian interview.

I wave him off, but as soon as I shut the door I feel
sad and lost. It's weird, we've been together 24/7 for
days now so suddenly being alone makes me feel
uneasy. So I decide to phone my best friend.

"Hi Nat, how are things. I miss you," says Cath. I'm
close to tears as I miss her too, but try and sound

brave, but she knows me too well. "You put too much pressure on yourself Nat. Make this work because I want to be out there too with you. I feel like a real saddo as I'm in mourning."

We chat for half an hour, both feeling slightly down, and finally I say I've got to go, things to do and all that, but it's because I'm afraid I might cry. All I need right now is to pop out for a coffee with her and have that warmth of familiarity for a second. I'm suddenly feeling so very grown up, weird to say that at my age, but being away from what you know, maybe that's what happens? It's not like I haven't been in this situation before, but this time, it feels long-term so it's kinda scary.

I get off the phone, have a bit of an ugly cry, and decide to pull myself together. Silly emotional me. I'm never ever normally like this.

I pop back online and I've got two replies from a national newspaper asking if I would be up for doing free restaurant reviews. Free food? Yes please. Another response from a property magazine I had contacted saying they would be keen to meet me to discuss my ideas, but that the editor is manic right now and could she phone me in a week. You see, there's always a light somewhere in the tunnel, and I am expecting a little much, too soon.

Now it's time to wait for Nathan and see how his interview went. I am super excited.

It's only 6pm, his interview was on the other side of town at 4pm, so I won't start worrying about him getting lost until after eight (mmmm, After Eight).

The trouble is we've become so reliant on our mobile phones, that I wonder what to do if he doesn't come back. When should I start panicking? What will I do if he doesn't come back? Nope, stop it, I can't think like that. Someone has been watching over us so far, so nothing can go wrong.

I decide to email my sister:

Hello my lovely sister, the bestest sis in the whole world ever!!!

Well, I woke up this morning and really missed you. It's so strange because I could go two weeks and not see you, but knowing you are so far away makes you think more. YOU HAVE TO MOVE TO CANADA!

Well, it's been quite an adventure so far. We got through immigration fine. They were being really harsh with some people, but were so lovely with us!

Then we stayed at my friends and the next day we got our SIN numbers and health insurance sorted, and it all happened so easily, no queues and everyone was saying "Welcome to Canada, great to have you here."

The following day we sorted out our banks and the transfers, and that went smoothly too. Then we went to the North Shore and started flat hunting. It's more expensive than we thought, but renting here is nuts. They put adverts in the paper in the morning and literally minutes later the places are taken.

Today (Saturday) we moved into our flat on West 4th. It's lovely. I have no idea what the area is like. I saw lots of graffiti outside, and thought Oh My God, but today we realised we are on the edge of Squamish Nation land, which I find so fascinating. One block up and there's all these posh houses, and across there are First Nations with their wooden eagle carvings, and then just down the road there are tramps...so we have rented a place for three months and will suss it out a bit more from there.

From our bedroom we have a view over the city, it's twinkling below us at the mo.

In our lounge we look one way and see Grouse Mountain, and the other we see the city...bliss.

We met everyone at Grouse on Thursday evening. We went up there and there was loads of snow already, but we're waiting for a huge dump so we can start work.

We got free food and chatted to loads of cool people. In fact everyone has been so helpful. I can't believe how they want to help out all the time.

Guess what too...I won a pair of snowshoes on Grouse when we were there on Thursday. My name was in a raffle and I won! It's the first time I have won anything!

Talk about luck, someone is looking over us.

The only thing that has shocked me so far is the cost of bedding. It's a nightmare to figure out when you're not used to it.

Well my lovely sis, I will keep you updated, and keep looking at the Okanagan as I think we will move there within the next year or so.

I send you lots of love and kisses and hugs,

Nats

Sometimes writing things down brings a bit of reality to the situation, about how much we've already achieved and how great people have been.

(November 23, 2007)

Oh yea, so snowboard instructing. It's time to start work at Grouse Mountain while still keeping an eye out for jobs in our chosen careers.

After the first day on the mountain, where I felt like a fish out of water, the days following suddenly start to feel a lot more normal. The last time I instructed was in Colorado, so it takes just a few sessions to adjust.

I start off by taking private lessons and drop-in lessons, and teaching everyone from a four-year-old kid to a 90-year-old man. Trust me, teaching a 90-year-old man to snowboard who has had a triple heart bypass and is only doing it to impress his 40-year-old girlfriend, well that ain't easy.

Then there's David Beckham's former personal trainer (or so he says), a big muscle of a man who can't stand on his snowboard and uses me to manoeuvre on the slopes. Boy was I ever bruised after that lesson. But nothing, and I mean nothing, prepared me for the zone camp. Cue dramatic music.

The "dreaded zone camp," as they are called within the instructors' circle, is a week of lessons with the same kids, eight hours a day. Basically during this time us instructors are glorified babysitters. Many parents who want to get rid of their children over the Christmas break will sign their kids up for ski/snowboarding lessons, whether they like it or not.

What you aren't told when you arrive in Vancouver as an instructor is that most of these kids are Korean. Lovely people, but it doesn't help when they don't understand a word you say, and you have a weird accent to boot (yes, that's me).

How can you explain mountain safety to a six-year-old Korean who only knows "yes' and "thank you" when they know you are seeking a response? And how can you tell that a parent understands that their child has run into a tree and may be suffering from concussion after being examined by ski patrol, when they reply "yes, thank you?"

Then again, there are the Starbucks gift cards that you tend to get given instead of tips, so it all makes it worthwhile, that and the $12 an hour….oh the life of an instructor.

Saying that, teaching is a lot of fun. Although I think I got away with it fairly lightly. Poor Nathan on the other hand had the girl who kept saying "I can do that" and clearly couldn't, and the Korean boys who actually came to blows on the slopes because of a misunderstanding in the language.

Then there's the differences in cultures. Korean men it seems are often treated like the alpha, and the women run around doing everything for them.

This results in many of the instructors having boys of 12 sat on the ground, pointing at their boots, grunting. This apparently translated means "do up my boots now." Needless to say they were quickly put in their place. But after a few days, tempers were wearing thin, on all sides.

If you could hear what the instructors say in the snow hut, you would be shocked. Maybe there should be a book entitled "What instructors say behind closed doors," or maybe not, as parents would never put their kids in ski school! But being the professionals they are, instructors walk out that door with a smile on their face, a lovely goggle tan, the patience of an absolute saint, and deliver the kids safely back to the parents at the end of the day. I have so much respect for instructors now.

Parents will of course be oblivious to the fact that the very same instructor lost five of his kids on the mountain in the fog the day before, because, well, we have one another's backs and, safety first and secrets second! After a week of 6am starts and babysitting children who constantly repeat, "can we go now," when another kid is clearly hurt, or ask "why do I need to turn?" "I'm tired," and yes, "can

I go now" again and again, it can start to get quite tiring. I feel for you teachers, I really do.

***

Chapter 7

WHAT'S THE DEAL BUD?

What's that smell? My gawd, it is everywhere. It's kind of sweet, kind of floral. Oh wait . . . its weed, you know, Mary Jane, Marijuana, and it is everywhere. This entire city smells of pot! And people seem to smoke it on the streets and no-one bats an eyelid. Or is it actual skunk? The smell of North Van.

I ask a few people what the laws are here regarding weed, and no-one seems to know exactly.

I've heard everything from it's legal, to you'll be thrown in jail if you're caught smoking it. Not that it makes a difference to me. I haven't tried it since I was teen, but my oh my, they are liberal here.

No wonder people seem so mellow. Now, where's the corner store, I need some munchies.

(Sidenote: As of October 18, 2018, subject to provincial or territorial restrictions, adults who are 18 years of age or older are legally able to possess up to 30 grams of legal cannabis, dried or equivalent in non-dried form in public, and share

up to 30 grams of legal cannabis with other adults.
Yup, the Cannabis Act is in force and as of October
17, 2019 Cannabis edible products and
concentrates will be legal for sale.)

***

Chapter 8

OUR FIRST VISITORS
(December 2007)

Our good friends Nina and Karl and their little girl
have come to stay. Yippee. A bit of familiarity.

The challenge, however, is that they've come when
we are mid zone camp and so we are completely
knackered. We are the worst hosts! I feel so sorry
for them. On top of that, we decide to move flats
mid stay because the apartment next door has come
up for rent and it is cheaper, and the downstairs
neighbours decide to put in a complaint because our
friend's little girl was bunny-hopping around the flat
at 7.30am. Come on people, she's a little girl and it's
past 7am!

Yes, we've moved. It was the biggest move of our
lives . . . to the flat next door. From one big move to
one tiny move. After telling the landlord we are not
getting as many hours as we had thought on the
mountain and that we need to find somewhere
cheaper, he tells us the flat next door, a one-
bedroom, is $600 cheaper, and available for rent. It
will also be great to get away from the landlord who
lives above us and partakes in some rather noisy

sessions, if you know what I mean. So we spend all of two hours carting our stuff next door, and finally settle into a flat I actually prefer.

Although it doesn't have the view of the city, it has a great view of the mountains, and the colourful graffiti opposite is really quite pretty. So Nathan and I set up a bed in the lounge and our friends take the bedroom, as it makes sense with us getting up early.

It's a tough couple of weeks, thanks to the zone camps, and our love of teaching is dimmed somewhat as we can't enjoy time with our friends. Although when I'm up on the mountains, looking down at the ocean below and the city in the distance, with Mount Baker ahead, I know I would much prefer to be in this "office" than in a concrete air-conditioned block.

This job has no real stress. You know, the usual work stress you encounter. The tiredness however is like something I've never experienced. You walk into the snow room and there are instructors sleeping on the benches. It's just hilarious. These are meant to be the ambassadors of the ski world; the athletes. Instead they are rubbing Deep Heat (or should that be RubA535) into their joints, catching up on sleep, and sneaking off for a fag, I mean cigarette (must stop saying that here), at any opportunity. I love snow school.

Unfortunately, that's not a passion felt by everyone.

I discover from a friend of ours in snowmaking that ski school is possibly the most hated department on the mountain. Apparently it's because many of the instructors are quite cocky and think they are above the other departments. This seems to have been missed by our group of people (unless I am oblivious to it), but I'm told this is an unusual year.

Day in the life of an instructor:

•Get up, have coffee.

•Get on the mountain, have a coffee.

•Take a kip on a bench, have a coffee.

•Fight over who wants to take the next lesson, as no-one can be bothered after having the morning off.

•Win the argument. Have a coffee.

•Head down from the mountain, grab a coffee.

Go home, watch Family Guy.

•Go to sleep.

•Wash. Rinse. Repeat.

(December 25, 2007)

It's Christmas Day! How exciting. A white Christmas.

As instructors, this is a busy time of year, so we head up the slopes, walk past Santa and his reindeers, no honestly, we do, and they are real (or the reindeers are anyway), and head to the ski hut.

It's a fun day as everyone is really excited, and we manage to get off work early, so we decide to do a few final runs with a new friend, Nick, (who is a Brit...so much for not mixing with our own). He has quite the fall and says he feels he has hurt his thumb.

We head inside and go for a bite to eat and as we sit there, Nick's thumb swells up to the size of a melon. Hmmmm. I think he may have broken it. So we send him off to A&E. But he's still smiling as the day, and the snow, have been amazing!

(New Year's Eve, 2007)

We are working.

We get home late and our friends are cooking king crab and we have the most amazing meal.

By 8pm we can hardly keep our eyes open. Oh lordy, our poor friends. As we lie in bed snoozing, I hear the faint cheers in the distance and our First Nation neighbours are banging drums outside. It must be midnight. I roll over and whisper to Nathan, "Happy first New Year in Canada baby."

***

Chapter 9

A DOLLAR IS ALL I NEED

It seems all we do is worry about money. And it is
kind of taking away from our experience in Canada.

We are desperately trying not to eat into our savings
that we worked so hard for so we can buy a house,
so we're living off our instructor's wage and eating
rice and vegetables. Hardly the diet of a snowboard
instructor. I'm losing weight fast and I don't like it.
I look like Skeletor.

And just when we think we've got it covered,
BANG along comes another bill. This time it's the
Medical Services Plan (MSP).

Books on Canada will tell you the health-care
system is like the NHS, as I've hinted at, but it's not
quite.

Thankfully, it's not quite like the US either.
Basically, you pay a small-ish fee online, which
covers you go to any doctors in BC. You don't even
need to register with them, you can just turn up, as
long as you have your medical card or a medical
number if your card hasn't come through.

You still have to pay for prescriptions, like the UK.
We get a bill through, as always at the wrong time,
for $288 for two months medical cover for Nathan
and I. That's not bad I know, but I wish we'd been
prepared. It's always a shock, especially when
you're living off rice. What I find out later from
friends is that some employers actually pay for this

with private healthcare, so yes, get yourself a job that covers it, that's for sure.

***

Chapter 10

WEDDING BELLS...EUROPE BOUND
(March 2008)

We're off to Austria for my sister's wedding! Oh my goodness, so exciting! I get to see my family again and see my beautiful sister get married.

We've only just arrived in Canada, but I promised my sister when we changed the date of moving to Vancouver, that come hell or high water, I would be there for her wedding.

It's expensive travelling to anywhere in Europe from Vancouver. A trip to Hawaii staying in a 5-star hotel? $235. A flight to Salzburg? $1,750. But it's my sister's wedding, so I don't care!

I'm so exited to be seeing my family in Austria.

We are in Austria, and it is absolutely magical.

On her big day my sister looks like an angel, Ben, my soon-to-be bro, looks so handsome and everything goes smoothly. I cried, my mum cried, my dad cried, my auntie cried, even some of the guests and their pets at the hotel cried. Being with my sister and my mum and dad, as well as my auntie and uncle from Germany, was just the best. In fact, I think I had more fun with them than I've ever had.

What an absolutely amazing day.

My sister, my beautiful, kind-hearted, sweet angel of a sister, is now married. Oh my heart sings for her. What an amazing family I have.

But . . . here comes the dreaded but . . .

Isn't it a shame how something can tarnish an experience. My thoughts right now are that I don't want to head back to Europe for quite some time. Not until the dust settles.

Why this sudden change of attitude after such an amazing time with my family and seeing my beautiful sister get married? Well, there were a few things that really upset the apple cart, as it were.

Just before we left, Nathan's dad's partner had left him.

The entire relationship left a bitter taste in Nathan's mouth and this news added to that. Of course, we felt guilty for leaving too, which might have been a catalyst for the anger. Afterall, his dad was alone now, and he hated being alone. It was all such a shock.

His partner's attitude seemed, from an outsider's point of view, to change overnight, or, in Nathan's eyes, as soon as we were no longer there to give the dad support. Easy to judge sometimes when you don't really know what's going on.

It transpires the partner had asked Nathan's dad to marry her (there's always more to a story than you see). He had said he didn't see a reason to get married and that he was still grieving, and that she had all the financial security she could have. Relationships, never simple, that's for sure. So we leave the country and she leaves the dad, and all this just before Christmas. Ouch. In Nathan's mind, it was ammunition. She had him by the short and curlies. I think that no matter what age you are, inside, you will still be a kid when it comes to things like this.

So, the last thing we had heard, his dad was single. People were rallying around. We had organized for him to join a gym, to get out there (not much help probably, but we were trying). Nathan was worried sick. Being so far away, what else can you do? Should he fly home? I couldn't tell him what to do, all I could do was stand by him and try and offer a little outsider's perspective.

My sister, as always, was right there, supporting as best she could, even trying to set his dad up with friends so he was not alone. My sister really is such an angel in that way, always looking out for others.

And so, for the wedding, we had agreed to share a room with his dad so he wouldn't be alone. It made sense. Then we could be sure he had company and also we could assess how he was coping.

Can you imagine our reaction then when he turned around just days before and said his girlfriend is coming now and we will all be sharing a family room. Oh goodness me...poor Nathan!

So when we get to Austria we stay with them in the same room, for one night. As an adult, no-one really wants to stay in the same room as the parents, even in the most ideal scenario. That same night Nathan's dad announced at dinner that they will be getting married, in three months! Oh no, not now, please not now. It's my sister's wedding. Couldn't they have waited until after? I can see Nathan's face is like thunder.

But, kudos to Nathan, he actually holds it together very well. He just goes quiet. As I settle in for the night in the put-me-up cot in the family room, I close my eyes and hear snoring from across the room. This week will be tricky. I am going to have to juggle Nathan's reaction, his dad and partner's reaction to his silence, and all this during what should be one of the most fabulous weeks of my sister's life. Shoot, to put it politely. Talk about bad timing.

I promise to myself I won't let my sister know any of this. It's her week and no-one, and I mean absolutely no-one, is going to ruin that.

The next day, Nathan decides to have a word with his dad. I realize neither of us has said congratulations. I think we are just in shock. We don't really have a grasp on the back story, and relationships can be complex. Who knows unless you are in the relationship what is actually going on. Maybe they truly do love each other afterall!

Nathan's chat turns out to be disastrous.

He tells his dad he believes they are marrying for the wrong reasons. His dad fuels the situation by saying he doesn't love her like he did the mother, which if you think about it is fair, but when you are the "child" comes across wrong...if there is even a right way to deliver that message.

Obviously things are awkward, which is an understatement by the way, and we can't stay in the same room we had booked, so Nathan and I try and find some hotels with vacancies. Fortunately my mum and dad help out, as always, they are my rocks, and we end up moving from one hotel to the next over the course of a week. Four hotels in total.

I keep telling myself to just think about how great the wedding was. Just think about dancing to Bavarian music with my Auntie; just think about messing around with my mum and dad and the family all doing crazy impressions as we got ready for the wedding with my sis in the bedroom; just think about riding on the horse-drawn carriage with my sister looking like a princess. Happy thoughts. Delete from my mind the gongshow that is going on around us.

On the way back to Canada, we are caught in a blizzard, get stuck on a train for 14 hours due to hurricane winds and end up surrounded by kids with swastikas on their jackets shouting at anyone who doesn't speak German at a train station in the middle of nowhere.

Think happy shiny thoughts. Release bad stupid thoughts.

I kiss the ground when we get back to Canada. Drama over, for now.

***

Chapter 11

LANGUAGE DIFFERENCES
(April, 2008)

Canadians call it self-assurance, self sales and survival, the Brits would often see it as arrogance and something to be frowned upon. I'm talking about the art of "selling yourself" to get a job, and I don't mean the red light kind.

Since arriving in Canada, I have gone through a path of enlightenment.

At first I thought all Canadians were just really amazing at their jobs. Well they told me so, so who am I to question them?

I have since been enlightened by my fellow Canadian friends.

I started to see cracks in that smooth plaster when I realized those same people who claimed to be amazing at their jobs, are what we call in Britain, winging it.

And on the numerous occasions when they were found out that they weren't doing their job, they had this incredible knack of passing the buck. I found this quite endearing; almost childlike, a kind of "it wasn't me, it was her" attitude. That was until the finger was pointed at me, and I had to correct the mistake and being me, wasn't quick enough to tell the person they were out of order. So I rectified that by telling the person later that we all make mistakes, but passing the buck just isn't on. An apology came soon after.

My friends keep trying to tell me that their main influence came from the US and British modesty isn't part of the culture.

But I honestly can't stand showing off, and that's exactly what I feel like I'm doing if I tell people what I've achieved and how well I can do my job. Yuk. Even writing that makes me feel nauseous. And yet, if I don't, it seems I will never be able to compete in this job market.

I start adjusting my cover letters for jobs. Instead of reading: "I would love to work with your company. I feel I have the experience and would love to join your team," I write, "As an award-winning journalist with 12 years experience, I have the abilities and skills to take your team to the next level. I would be an asset to your company." Yuk, pass me the bucket, I am going to throw up.

It seems to be getting the results though, so now I am trying to change my attitude, without allowing myself to sound bolshy or brash. Not easy I tell you, but when in Rome.

I love Canada, and what I'm starting to realize is that Canadians can be quite blunt.

If being told by your supervisor that your partner gets better classes than you because basically he likes him better isn't blunt, what is?

I suppose it's better than back biting, but getting used to this is going to take some adjustment.

Nathan is sarcastic by nature, and that has been remarked upon, but the bluntness and the tendency of some to put you down to lift themselves up is remarkable and can be, well, hurtful.

I'm learning quickly, and realize that my thin skin won't do me any favours out here. I'm used to hanging around with gentle folk who suffer from that horrid Catholic guilt thing, you know the kind where anytime you say something mean or think of anything horrible, you go through 40 days and 40 nights of mental whipping for being so darned evil.

It seems the Canadians I've encountered so far have a far more upfront attitude.

I kind of like them for it though, because they can take as good as they give. As soon as you stand your ground they back down and become lovely again. It's like being in the animal kingdom.

***

Chapter 12

BUYING A CAR IN VANCOUVER
(April 2008)

Now, I'm pretty sure if Jeremy Clarkson were to start this chapter he'd probably say something witty about cars in the Great White North, probably including some political agenda and a dig at caravans.

Me, I'm no Clarkson, just your average girl when it comes to cars, and a dash of whatever I have learned from my man over the years. If a car gets me from A to B then I'm happy. And yet something strange has happened to me since moving to Vancouver. I used to like my small cars, not the Ford Ka kind, more the VW Polo or Golf (a Rabbit over here), although I admit my favourite car aside from my Green Golf that I called Humphrey Bogey, was my Rover Metro. I didn't care who took the piss out of that car, it was beautiful to me. Go ahead, make all the jokes you want.

But as I was saying, something has happened to me.

My head no longer turns when I see a car. Now I strive to own an SUV, that's a sports utility vehicle and to many of us Brits, one of those massive cars you usually only see in North America.

If you don't own something that weighs around three tonnes here, you are basically overlooked on the road. And on these roads, where Canadians have been known to run over anything they don't like (just check out the March 08 newspaper headlines *'Arrest Made in Canada Road Rage Death' United Press International*; *'Police arrest suspect in B.C Road Rage Death', CBC*, and so on), owning a big truck comes in very handy.

So yes, my taste has changed. I now look at the 4x4 not as a wagon for married mothers to cart their children over those rugged Bournemouth town centre roads, but as a cool part of Canadian life. And I even have a reason for wanting to own a gas guzzling machine, with these harsh winters and rough interior roads. The east coast of Canada is laughing at me for saying that right now. West coast softies that we are with our tropical weather.

So it's time to buy a car.

We've gone for four months using public transport, and although TransLink seems pretty amazing with ithe monthly card that seems to get you anywhere, at any time, there's no beating having your own mode of transport.

Taking the bus has made me feel like a student, and I've enjoyed that. I've also enjoyed the interaction with people from all walks of life.

My friend recently said that after returning to the UK from her visit to Canada, that she got on a bus with her three year-old daughter, and she had got so used to chatting to people on the buses here and tried to continue with this in England. Unfortunately she received a very rude response from all passengers, which prompted my friend to say "Darling, we are in England now. People are rude here." I think it's just that people in larger towns aren't used to it, so it makes them a bit suspicious.

There are, however, downfalls of public transport. The biggest one being that it takes four hours to get from North Vancouver to downtown and back – when in fact it's just a 20 minute car journey. This of course takes into account walking time, waiting for the sea bus, the bus to the next destination and so on.

The second thing about public transport is that you see things you wish you hadn't. Like the lady who sat opposite me picking her nose for the entire 25 minutes and wiping it across her face and the hand pole next to her, while staring straight at me. Was it rude that I averted my gaze?

So yes, it was time for a car.

Personally, I'd grown to love the Jeep Cherokee or the Rav4. Nathan however was keen on the Toyota 4runner or the Nissan Pathfinder.

Would it be a battle of wills? Of course not! In our house, cars are Nathan's pleasure.

But it wouldn't be that simple.

In BC the Insurance Corporation of British Columbia (ICBC) is a provincial crown corporation and to get the basic coverage you have to go through them. No competition means high fees. Also, as we found out it's not really about the size of the engine, but more about whether it's an import, the colour of the car, number of doors, whether it's a station-wagon (a lot more expensive), number of coffee cups (I made that one up) and so on. A lot of it boils down to the crash ratings and cars most stolen, which ICBC gives you a breakdown on.

It turns out that the Chrysler Caravan/Voyager is number one in 2006 and the Jeep Cherokee comes in at number six. Hmmm.

Having heard various stories about how expensive insurance is before we came, I had my insurance company print off an official form saying I had nine years no claims. This seems to come in very handy, especially considering Nathan has had company cars and only has one year's official no claims.

So we decide to make the call. We've been told not to go directly through ICBC as they will quote you the full works, and that there is another way. By going through an independent broker they will tell you what packages to put onto the ICBC basic coverage that you are required to have by law.

So we phone up a lady at Canadian Direct who has been recommended and she patiently takes us through the best cars to go for. I say we, I mean Nathan. It's his forte here, as I really have no clue what I'm talking about. It turns out that the cars we are looking at all come to around the same; around the $1,800 mark for a year's insurance. Gulp.

Coming from the UK that seems really steep, but you've got to remember that cars, petrol (or gas), servicing...all these are a lot cheaper, so it kind of balances out in the end, right?

So, what car? Where do you start? The marketplace is saturated with used car dealers, and then there's all the local classifieds and of course Craigslist (I suppose it's the Canadian version of ebay).

I leave that to Nathan, and it takes him a few weeks to go through the "should I, shouldn't I" process. Eventually, after talking to people, it seems the Toyota 4Runner and the Nissan Pathfinder are indeed the more dependable cars, so we decide to focus our attention on those.

It all happens so quickly. Friday night we see one on Craigslist, we phone the number and the man at the other end of the phone says he has two kids and is looking to sell as he has no need for a "camping car" at the moment.

We take the bus, take a look, and decide we will have it. Yup, just like that. Some may say it was wreckless (pun intended), but the car looked in great condition, Nathan was smiling, it was in our price range ($4,000) and the guy seemed pretty genuine. In the end, a car is a car, it could go wrong tomorrow or in five years, who knows. The joy of buying used. So we've got ourselves a car . . . oh, and no insurance or driving license as yet, aside from our UK driving licence, which you can only drive on for 90 days.

In Canada, when you buy a used car, you head down to the local ICBC office with the current owner to do the paperwork. Well, that's what they say. In fact it's probably because you get charged taxes on the price of the car, which puts an extra $308 on the price of our car. But we did manage to insure it for the day, so we were able to shake hands and store it at our friends garage, only to see it the following week, when we finally sorted out our insurance. Oh my goodness, we've bought a car, and already we've named it Emily. I don't know why; it just suits her.

(Sidenote: ICBC's Autoplan insurance is sold exclusively through its province-wide network of 900 Autoplan brokers. I definitely recommend finding a broker! If you or a member of the household has owned a driver's licence for 10 years or more you can be put on the insurance.)

***

Chapter 13

INSTRUCTOR HELL
(Still April 2008)

Back to Grouse Mountain and instructing.

Friends have come to visit. Well, they've come to visit their brother, which is even better as we can truly enjoy their company, because we are pretty much still settling in and all over the place right now.

We've arranged to meet for dinner on Saturday. I love this, it's like being back in the UK, only, despite all the lessons, we are actually feeling really really happy here now!

Spring Break. A time for wild parties. A time to let your hair down and go nuts.

That's the impression American movies have given us anyway. Maybe that's true . . . unless of course you're a ski/snowboarding instructor. Holy Schmidt.

Spring Break for instructors means, as I've said before and am at risk of sounding like a broken record, being a glorified babysitter, pushing your sanity to the limit, and the one time you can get guaranteed pay due to the long hours. Yippee.

If you're lucky, you'll get a group of kids who want to learn, but who have the capabilities of a tranquilized turtle. If you're unlucky, you get a dozen little shits who pretend to have ADHD, the manners of someone who has been cryogenically frozen since Caveman days, and the testosterone to match...that's girls and boys.

Yes, I've just experienced three days, that's 24 hours of hell. And I've still got 16 hours to go.

I should have known.

The parents drop their children off in the morning for the school snowboard camp, and actually give me a look in their eyes . . . is that pity? Oh no, what was I in for? I felt like a lamb being led to slaughter.

What followed was bullying among the children, ice rocks being thrown at my head, pushing, shoving, children getting lost in the mist on the mountain, need I go on? I think parents right now will be nodding their heads.

Admittedly there were three kids who were like a disease and rubbed the others up the wrong way. I blame the parents (isn't that what you are meant to say)?

At one point, one of the children, originally from China asked, "Are you from England? English are all racist and hate Asians." When I asked him where he got that notion from, he said his father. Interesting. Well for that I think it's fair to say I can blame the parents.

This also explains why he had been saying "no" to everything I politely asked him to do all morning, why he'd thrown the biggest ice clumps at me, despite numerous times telling him not to and the dangers, and why he turned round to me at one point and said "I've decided I hate you."

At that point I felt like grabbing his head and shoving his face in the snow making him into a tiny human snowcone. I could always tell the parent he had tripped, couldn't I? Before you call the authorities, of course being a "professional," I didn't. Instead I said "I gathered. You've been giving me attitude all day, but do I seriously look like someone who [gives a shit] cares. I'm here to teach you and if you refuse to learn I can move you to another group tomorrow. That's fine."

I have realized it's like a battle of wills with children. But not having your own you forget this power struggle thing kids have.

The other children in the group started laughing saying he will probably end up with a really mean instructor and it serves him right. Well that was the start of a dramatically different child. He started snowboarding close to me, asking me what I wanted him to do, and telling me he does like me, it's just my nickname that the kids had given me he didn't like (Apple) and that if I was a Golden Delicious, he actually would like me. I think that's fair. Oh dear, was that my heart melting just a little?

That evening, all us instructors head off to a local bar and order 15 pitchers of beer. You should have heard the conversation around the table! "I will never have children," I declared, and was joined by countless nods. I totally respect both parents and teachers, even if they are a little mad for opting to have these blood sucking beasts. I joke of course.

There had been fights, broken bones and one child had even started to hit an instructor. It was time to go home, lie down, and dream of a child-free zone.

The next morning, feeling drained, I slowly, very slowly, walk towards my group. One of the mothers comes up to me to tell me her kids, the very same ones with the attitude, had woken up very grouchy and she was sorry.

I had to use everything in my power not to jump up and down with joy. Woohoo, someone is looking over me. Fortunately the other kids were better mannered, but had decided to start bullying tactics on another child. And so the week continued.

I'm a bit of a soft touch, but at times even I lost my rag.

It turns out the children even fight over who is sitting next to me on the chair lifts. Children. I will never understand them. Unless you are a teacher, or have been a ski/snowboard instructor, seriously, I don't think you'll never understand the pain we go through for so little pay. Oh, or a parent, yes, if you are parent and they do it for free, although I suppose they are your own.

For us snowboarders, I think it's a sign that we must really love the sport, or the kids in the end.

The week resulted in even the instructors who didn't smoke, sliding off behind the shed for a sneaky fag!

***

Chapter 14

TRUST ISSUES, ME? JEEZ

OK. So I think, in fact I know, I have trust issues.

The friend I mentioned earlier who used very clever mental bullying tactics (I hate to use the word, but that's what it felt like at that age) scarred me when it came to friends, because it takes a while for me to actually trust friends. Crazy how small things impact us. Thank you Cath for coming into my life and re-training me and teaching me girls can be awesome!

With girls, it seems you just have to be so careful, because you turn your back and they'll steal your man or bitch to another friend about you not being available that one time. I know, I know, that's a horrible stereotype, but considering the number of people I know who have experienced this, what am I meant to think?

Needless to say, I've shied away from anyone I think may be like that and high maintenance; the ones who get snippy if you don't call or text back immediately . . . they are just not my kind of people.

I don't know how many people can say they have a true friend, one they can trust implicitly. I have one I know of for sure. I have zero doubt about that. You're lucky when you find one.

So coming to Canada I decided that although I really love being around people and make friends pretty easily, finding true friends, who would put their hand in fire for you, would mean I needed to leave that baggage behind. Well, if I managed to find some super solid girlfriends in the UK, surely I could in Canada, right. Right?

And I decided I needed to make female friends. I warm to guys more, just because I love that witty banter, taking the piss, and I'm not a girlie girl. My bathroom has more tools in it than product. But out of respect for Nathan I decide it isn't fair to have all male friends, and so far, I've met some pretty awesome guys who I've forced upon Nathan! Here, take this one, he's cool.

So I had gotten really quite close to a couple of girls, who were a great laugh. We could fool around together and one in particular had a wacky sense of humour like mine. We just seemed to click!

However, I could still feel that element of mistrust from me, that baggage that was so heavy, dragging me down. What a way to live. It's all about balance, right? Time to grow up.

It doesn't help when new friends constantly make comments about your other half and tell you they have photos of him on their computer. Are they joking? Is this normal behaviour? Personally, it's not something I would even think of saying, but maybe it is normal here to joke about it?

Ok, ok, so I am sure someone who was actually thinking that wouldn't say that? But you just don't know.

Am I being a paranoid android? Is this actually normal? Was it me with that 40 tonne backpack of mistrust? Should I be worried? But why would I? I can trust Nathan. Uggghhhhhh. It's like starting a new relationship, you carry all this baggage and have to figure out what is yours and what is theirs.

Relationships....oi vey.

At this very moment I want to transport my UK friends over here. I just adore them. I feel like I am back at school. I honestly need to grow up.

If only I had a handle on what Canadian girls were like, maybe I would understand this behaviour better? Then again, are women all that different worldwide? Won't there always be some that wants what someone else has and thinks it could be better if it were theirs.

Right, I think it's time for me to allow benefit of the doubt take the lead and just see where that takes me.

Only time will tell I suppose, and it's all part of our Canadian experience…

***

Chapter 15

MOANING BRITS

It should have been Friday the 13th. It wasn't. It was Good Friday, but there was nothing good about it.

The day started off badly. Getting up at 5:30am is never good when you're not a morning person to begin with. Just as we were walking to the bus stop we had one of those lightbulb moments when you realize the buses are on a holiday bus timetable. Oh crap!

This meant whatever we decided to do, we would arrive late. Unless we took a cab and at $25 for the ride (that's two hours pay) we weren't really in a position to part with that cash. We didn't yet have full insurance for our car either, so there was that.

Being this close to the end of the season, the previous months panic of being late had left us and we shrugged our shoulders and decided to walk the five blocks across and eight blocks up to see if the other bus would be arriving anywhere near our 7.45am start.

Sweating before you even got to start eight hours of snowboarding isn't the best, but then again, if you've ever walked in snowboarding boots, ski pants and a thick jacket, you'll get the image of what we looked like after walking 25 minutes uphill.

So that was the start.

When we arrived at the base of the mountain, we weren't alone. There had been a major accident on one of the bridges. The bridges, the bane of everyone's existence who commutes to or from the North Shore.

From there the day just got so, so much better…oh wait, no it didn't.

Fortunately, the kids had decided to behave and decided that today they loved me. Other instructors weren't so lucky. The worst incident of the day had to be when one of the instructors sent her children up on the chairlift and one dropped his goggles. He, of course, I mean why wouldn't you, decided his best option was to jump from the lift and retrieve them. The other children on the lift held down the safety bar and told him not to do it. After five minutes he managed to slide under the safety bar and launch himself from what was the equivalent of a four-storey building.

I had wondered what was going on when I saw a large group of ski patrollers surrounding a child on the floor. I would never imagine anyone, let alone a 13-year-old child, could actually be that, well stupid.

He was lucky.

The past week had been "puking" (apparently a Quebecois phrase for dumping with snow), so he'd landed on soft powder and all was OK. Had that been one week earlier, that same spot had been sheet ice, and it would have been a very different outcome.

After a few great runs down double blacks (oh yea, the rating system differs here quite a bit from Europe, in that a double black is more like a red in Europe), where I'd got my kicks when my children had been hounding me to ride on the steeper slopes and I demonstrated how to turn and then sent them down one by one. Of course only a few managed it, but watching them tumble down reminded me of my first experience on blacks. Throwing them in at the deep end! It's a bit of a leveller, that's for sure.

I would consider myself to be a responsible instructor. No seriously. I'm not kidding you. I've seen children who can only snowplough guided down the black runs just because an instructor wants to enjoy fresh tracks.

Anyway, it all went sour again.

There was the ski lift that broke down. Four of my kids had got on the lift, and I was just about to get on with the other two (I'd lost one earlier in the day, not literally you understand, although by now that probably wouldn't shock you – she'd gone to Whistler with her dad for the weekend) when the lift creaked to a stop.

This was no ordinary mechanical problem. Apparently the brake that slows the lift at the top had broken and the lift had swung back 10 feet.

This took 55 minutes to repair, and if you know what kids are like waiting, well it was crazy. No matter how many times you explain what's going on they still ask, "why are we waiting? Why can't we go?" "Can I jump down?"

You could tell them that if we go everyone will die, and they will still turn around two minutes later and ask: "Why can't we go"?

So to pass the time, snowball fights ensued. Kids were sent into the trees to relieve themselves (it seems this isn't commonplace for most kids out here) and the BC smell I had mentioned earlier wafted through the air. One eight-year-old child shouted: "Yuk, I can smell pot," I mean how the hell do they know these things? I am getting old.

When the chair started working we were asked to wait in case it broke again. So I had four extremely hyperactive children at the top of the mountain, aged five to 11. I did give them an energy bar as they were hungry, so I suppose there's that.

I advised ski patrol, who asked if I thought my kids would wait for me. My reply? "Kids have a short attention span. Any longer than 10 minutes and nothing is certain."

Fortunately, they managed to radio to the top station, and another instructor took them down the mountain.

The day can be summed up by saying kid went missing, instructors yelled constantly at children for throwing ice snowballs, there were lots of bumps and bruises, and there was a look of pure pain and exhaustion on all the instructors faces.

So what do instructors do after a difficult week? Meditate? Ride it out? Nope, head to the local bar, order 15 pitchers of beer, smoke more cigarettes than we care to admit and eat chicken wings and just, well, let rip.

The day ended amazingly and the camaraderie, even with the one we call Umpa Lumpa, (given to him as he has short man syndrome, and possibly the only unlikable character on the mountain, but we still welcomed him along) was like nothing I've ever experienced. The night resulted in people showing off their party tricks which included everything from dislocating shoulders to Donald Duck impressions.

Instructing...if it doesn't kill you, it will send you nuts.

**

Chapter 16

A GERMAN, A POLE AND A JEW WALK INTO A BAR

It seems my Canadian female friends are turning out to be very caring and loyal. Sarcastic? Yes. A little harsh at times? Yes. But my God they are caring. So far, my closest friends are a Pole, a Jew and then there's me, a German.

And no, that's not the start of a bad joke . . . well not yet anyway.

**

Chapter 17

CAR INSURANCE DRAMA

Back to the car. It seems that no matter how much research and preparation you do when you're emigrating, you can guarantee there will always be a glitch in your well-laid-out plans.

We thought we had been cautious. We'd ticked all the boxes on every "what to do when you emigrate" website/book/list we had managed to get our hands on, so we were kind of over-confident when it came to insuring a car . . .especially after our previous conversation when we originally bought the car.

We knew the price was going to be extortionate, but we'd been told if you had a letter from your insurance company saying you had more than eight years no claims, then you would get a whopping 40 percent off. That's quite a lot when you're looking at insurance of around $3,000 a year. And as we'd both driven for more than 10 years, we were also entitled to an extra discount.

So we woke up on Saturday, after the week of hell with crazy kids, and we were like those hyperactive children as we looked up the route to New Westminster where Emily, the lady who was dealing with our insurance, would be waiting for us. Ironic I know that she would have the same name as the one we gave the car. It was a sign, surely!

We popped into the office and asked the girl behind the counter to print off the letter we had received from my previous insurance company in the UK that reaffirmed my clean driving record and years of no claims.

When we turned up to see Emily, she took a look at the letter and said she didn't think ICBC would accept it, as I didn't have a letter from each and every insurance company from the past eight years, and the insurance had gaps in it as I had lived abroad during that time period.

Now, if you know British car insurance, you'll know that every year, when most people get their renewal letter, most people will take a look online to see if there is a cheaper option out there. And then you end up flip-flopping between insurance companies in order to play the "who will give me the best deal, because I'm an awesome driver" game.

That normally means that because British companies tend to miss out on the trick of keeping hold of their customers by offering them a deal, many of us go elsewhere. It also means that I have to contact eight individual companies, located in anywhere from John O Groats to Lands End, and try and get hold of someone who still has my policy number from the year 2000, and more importantly, would be willing to print out a letter to say I had a year's no claims and then fax it across.

Getting someone to do that when you are face-to-face is difficult enough, but when you are 5,000 miles away, claiming to be someone and convincing them it isn't a case of identity fraud, well that's about as easy as getting Gordon Ramsay to stop swearing for a day.

Nathan's face fell.

He went from elated to deflated.

Poor Emily! Poor Nathan. Poor us!

She saw the disappointment and suggested we get on the case asap. Emily went on to say that maybe we could insure the car for three months and that would give us enough time to get the letters, and that if we had any trouble she would get onto them. People are just so darned helpful!

Then she said we could come back and she would waive the transfer fee. It was better than nothing, and anyway, what else could we do, rules were rules. We weren't going to burden my sister with the task of getting onto the insurance companies. It's hard enough when you have to do it for yourself.

I'd learned when my parents emigrated to Spain and we had to handle various companies who thought we were fraudsters when we were just trying to prove we had the authority to act on their behalf and weren't after their inheritance. Having experienced that, I had vowed to leave no stones unturned, but, as we were quickly learning, it's not always possible.

So we left the insurance company with our BC Olympic license plates in our hands ($20 more for the beautiful mountain picture, but well worth because it is just so darn pretty) and we went for a semi-celebratory coffee.

That evening we met some English friends for dinner in Edgemont Village in North Vancouver. We took the bus. Ironic I know, but don't drink and drive.

It was an amazing evening. The British sense of humour is something you really do learn to appreciate when you are away, but I am starting to see that there is a negative streak with us Brits and a tendency to put ourselves down. This concept is starting to become a little alien to me already. Already?

What is it about Britain that makes people think they are useless, and don't have the skills to progress? And from my experience, they can be so hard working. It's something I don't miss, but that unfortunately I still have. I'm a work in progress, that's for sure.

It's so great having a car. Things that usually take us four hours, now take 20 minutes.

Today we managed to visit Deep Cove, an amazing area to the east of North Vancouver where people go kayaking. Traditionally it was a clamming and fishing area of the Tsleil-Waututh nation. Then we drive around Lynn Valley, another cute neighbourhood in North Vancouver, and up Capilano Road toward Grouse Mountain, AND we get the food shopping, all within four hours.

How did we get on without a car? How did I become so spoiled?

When we get home, we have a message from our boss at the mountain to ask if we could we be there for 7.30am. Before our car days, that would have meant we would have had to get up just after 5am to catch the bus. Not now we have a car.

No worries!

***

Chapter 18

MORE LESSONS ABOUT INSTRUCTOR LIFE

I am such a spooner.

I have been the one to give instructors "the look" when I've seen them taking children who are far from capable down black runs, just because they didn't want to miss out on the fresh powder. So what do I go and do? I decide to listen to some advice to take my very capable student down a tree line off the side of a double black diamond run. An area the instructors often go down, but which I had yet to explore.

Now if you know mountain orientation, you know that's not wise. Not wise at all. And if you know my orientation skills on a mountain and my ability to seek out the less than idyllic areas, then you know that's about as wise as entering a lion's den. There's was the one time I fell in a creek, oh wait, that wasn't an isolated incident.

But today I am riding with a girl who is a seriously strong rider.

We've had an amazing morning building a kicker off a run in a powder bowl, and although it's not the best kicker by any stretch of the imagination, she is happy because it's ours and only we know it's there. Well us and the hikers who use the trail, even though it's not open in the winter due to avalanches.

Actually it was quite funny, while we were sat in the trees we heard a hiker say "what the hell" – he then looked at us and asked "did you build this?" Considering we were sat next to it with a shovel, we couldn't exactly deny the small mountain we had created. We giggled. Instructing often brings the kid out in you.

Anyway, so off we go into the trees to find this perfect tree run everyone has been telling me about.

I think I'm being sensible by taking a route that stays close to the run, but we get a bit carried away. The next minute, my student speeds off in another direction. I yell at her to stop, and ask what's in front of her. The reply? "A cliff, I think?"

I shout at her to stay where she is and make my way through the trees to where she's stood.

On the tree in front of her is a sign that says CLIFF! I peer over and sure enough there's a sheer drop.

It seems no matter where we look, there's a cliff. Shoot! (To put it politely.)

Now, this isn't the first time I've found myself in this kind of situation, but normally I'm with friends, and I've relied on stronger riders to get us out of it.

Today I am an instructor, with a student, and her safety is in my hands.

It's funny how at times like these you find the Rambo within. I see to my left that a part of the cliff slopes away at a 75 degree angle and is covered in ice. Below it is a powder field.

We have two choices: either make my way down there, or take our boards off and try and hike back up, which can be the more dangerous option as the trees are tightly packed, the snow is icy, and the chances of slipping are high. Very high.

So I scoot across and see a small tunnel leading down to the run that we could fit through.
It all happens to fast. As I whip down I notice a branch across the tunnel and grab it, softening the blow and yanking my wrist at the same time.

I'm home and dry, but my sweet student is above me. I could either go down and call ski patrol, and leave my student alone and scared. Or I could find a safe route for my student to come down. I weigh up the options.

If I stay at the bottom I can grab her. So in a calm voice I persuade her to slip down. She tells me she's scared, and she's not sure what to do. I know that feeling. I have been such an idiot. But I know she will be safe this way.

I calmly talk her through what she needs to do, where she needs to aim, and persuade her it will be fine and that I'm here for her.

She tells me she's on her toe edge, which means she's face down. She has a helmet on which is good, but I'm worried she will hurt her face, so I tell her she must use the edges of her board to slow herself down.

What is just minutes seems like hours, but finally she decides to let go and slide down. I grab her and she lands into a pile of powder. I check about 20 times to see if she is OK and if anything is hurt. She assures me she is fine and suddenly shrieks "that was so cool!" Well, that's one word for it.

We look back up at the cliff. One inch further and I daren't even think what could have happened.

I'm such an idiot. Never again.

We make our way down, and discover three young boys with their boards off who had taken a wrong turn and ended up on the other side to where we were. One had let go of his snowboard and it had gone shooting down the mountain, never to be seen again.

We get to the bottom and call ski patrol to make sure they are OK.

Then the entire situation dawns on us. My student gets hysterical with laughter. I am in shock. I feel so very irresponsible and thank my lucky stars that I am in fact so, well lucky.

We do a few more runs and when we say goodbye at the end of the day, my student gives me a wink and tells me I'm the best instructor ever. I definitely don't think so at this point.

That night, as I sit nursing my left hand which has decide to swell up to the size of a water balloon, I think if that's karma working her magic, then I deserve it. Snowboarding really does resemble life. Sometimes you need to weigh up the risks and take the unknown, yet safest route.

It turns out I'm not alone in leading myself or students to that area. I talk to various instructors who say, "Oh, I've been there. There's only a few ways out and they are scary."

Another instructor, who I thought was Mr Sensible says: "I made that same mistake and one of my students shot down a part of the cliff. Fortunately she was OK. I've managed to keep that quiet. I've discovered a great path through there that you can go down though. Want to join me and my kids tomorrow?"

Why not!

They say you live and learn. I don't think so. You just get more stupid with age.

The trouble with being a snowboard instructor is, having snowboarded in a "technical way" for so long, it can lose its appeal.

I want to feel free again. I want to ride how I want to ride, to jump off things and tumble and not care if anyone sees me. I want to act like an idiot, catch an edge, land on the nose of my board and not care about weight distribution on the snowboard or shoulder positioning.

I can't.

If I ride slightly off balance, I feel as if I am being scrutinized by, well, myself. And when your husband turns around to you in a lesson and tells you your jumps suck – and all this in front of students you are meant to be training, well that kind of knocks your confidence and makes you feel like you shouldn't be teaching.

In truth, I'm tired of being told, you ride too much like this, or you can't do that. I want to be able to just have a laugh. Riding 90 days full-on as an instructor can take away that sense of freedom and fun you seek with snowboarding.

I just want to be on a mountain, with people who don't care if you can't pull off a trick and don't make you feel crappy if you fail. I do hope instructing hasn't ruined my love of the one sport I've felt truly passionate about my entire life.

Next day....

Scrap that! It has been dumping with snow. It's our first day off in quite some time, and we are up at 6.30am to catch the first tram up the mountain.

We head straight into the glades on the black run where I encountered the cliff. It's amazing. I feel wild and free again as I glide around one tree and then another.

Then we head off-piste to a place that locals call poop shoots. Interesting name. The reason is that it is how you feel when you get there! Take a wrong turn and you're facing a 20-foot drop down to the next skiable area.

What an amazing morning. I love snowboarding again. Seems I just needed a day off. I was bloody knackered, as all instructors are.

Riding with Nathan is amazing too. He ieaves his instructor side at home too and I feel in safe hands. With his natural mountain instinct I am able to clear my mind, blow out the cobwebs, and feel free as a bird.

Wow. Powder days; that's what snowboarding is about. Oh yes, that's why we are here.

(Sidenote: North Shore Rescue are our heroes in Vancouver. They offer a variety of search and rescue services – the main ones being; mountain search and rescue; helicopter rescue; urban search and rescue; public education; and civil emergency response. There is no charge for these services of the team. If you find yourself in trouble on the mountains and wish to contact the team for a search and rescue emergency, dial 9-1-1 and ask for the police. But just go prepared and don't put yourself in a situation where you will put extra strain on these amazing volunteers.)

***

Chapter 19

HOW VERY TAXING
(Yup, still April 2008)

I'm sorry, what? We have to do our own taxes?
Nooooo! We have to fill in more forms . . . and
numbers, but I'm not a numbers person. I deal with
words, numbers freak me out. I am sure I have
number dyslexia. Help me...

I'm also employed by a company. I'm not self
employed. How? What? Why? So many questions!
The only time I ever had any dealings with my taxes
in the UK was, well, never. I honestly can't
remember ever having to touch them. My employer
and the accountant magically took care of deducting
my income tax and national insurance from my
wages (as I would sadly see a huge chunk disappear
out of my monthly wage packet on the slip) and
then, miraculously, if at the end of the year I
somehow overpaid, I would get a tax rebate.
Winner!

But now I find myself faced with something called
a T4 and I have to file my own taxes. I don't get it. I
know, I know, when in Rome at all that jazz, but
just like the UK my payslips have a nice chunk
taken off the initial and more appealing figure
which goes towards goodness knows what and who
knows where (pensions, haha, as if they will exist
when I finally get to retire at the age of 95). So is
someone not doing their job here? Yikes.

In truth, it's just the idea of having to go through all
those numbers and having to hook out my payslips,
(what's my password again to log in to that system

we have at work)? How dull. I think that is my biggest gripe. I just find taxes so dull!

Having spent months, no I take that back, years, gathering information that we needed to get our permanent residency, I thought I was done with that kind of paperwork. Adulting. Bah.

It turns out that you need to file taxes by the end of April, and the tax year runs from January to January. I think.

So, what's this T4? It sounds like a Star Wars character, and in many ways, the similarities are there. I mean its pretty alien and I am not sure how it works, and it is creating all these bips and bop sounds in my head.

The T4 quite clearly, once you figure it out that is, is a slip prepared by my employers to summarize how much money I earned, how much income tax was deducted... zzzzzzzz, sorry I just fell asleep.

OK, time to quit moaning like an old b**tard and figure out the cheapest way, I mean simplest way I can do this, and hope we don't owe any money.

First stop online. So apparently you can file your taxes online. Yay. Unless this is your first time, in which case you can't. Boo. I feel like I am in some kind of Punch and Judy show.

The Canada Revenue Agency website isn't the easiest to navigate, either. But eventually, after about two hours, I find the page (I think) that I need.

I download the forms so I can sit down and figure this out. The forms are actually pretty straight-forward, but I didn't realize you can claim back things like medical, transportation costs and other work-related costs. Does a two-four count (I hope you like my use of Canadiana here. Just trying to fit in. And for those of you from the UK, a two-four is 24 beer bottles. A bit like what we call a six pack...only four times that amount because Canadians must be hardcore or something, well they have to be considering the price of alcohol in this province).

It seems there are a number of ways I can go about this. I can use a variety of tax software online that will do the calculations for me and costs around $15, then I can print off the forms and send them in to the Canada Revenue Agency by snail mail, or I can use an accountant, which costs, wait, hang on, nope, I can't find it.

So I decide to ask around. A few friends suggest using TurboTax software (ooh look #1 Tax software, it has got to be good), or, to pop into H&R Block (love the name).

I hear all these horror stories that if you don't fill the forms out correctly, the Big Boys from the tax office will hunt you down. I have images of me typing in a wrong number and being hounded by Dog The Bounty Hunter. I don't want a criminal record. I want to stay in Canada. There's something about numbers, they just kind of freak me out. Have I said that already? I have no idea where this came from. I was really quite good at math at school. I remember loving solving mathematical puzzles. We would sit around a horseshoe table and I would happily figure out the conundrum and then my mates would ask me for the answer, and I would again happily oblige.

But there was that one time during the MOC exams where my brain just left the building. I blanked. Kind of like a panic attack. I'm not sure what happened, except that I sat there staring at the exam papers in front of me and there was nothing, and I mean nothing in my head. I couldn't read what was on the page. It was a jumble of words and signs, and nothing. I sat there for the hour and then handed my paper in. Nothing I tell you.

My math teacher pulled me aside a few days later and asked me what went wrong, and I told him I had no clue. He was really sweet about it. I think he knew I must have had some kind of panic attack, but he just said, "It's OK. You'll be fine during the actual exam." He was a good sort. He was right.

So maybe that's where this number phobia comes from. Who knows. All I know is, I'm not a fan of numbers. I love words. Again, have I said that already?

So if I can hand this over to someone else, then I will. And of course, being the wife, paperwork falls in my "Honey To-Do" list. So I decide to suck it up and go back to TurboTax.

You know what? It's actually pretty simple, but I still have no real idea about what we can claim for. Apparently, you can't claim for individual bus tickets, but you can for a monthly pass. Had we known, we would have chosen the monthly pass and actually kept the receipts. Oh bugger. And I pride myself on my research skills. I am rolling my eyes at myself as we speak.

There's something on the forms about an RRSP, which apparently, if you're smart, you have one. So I do some research. Apparently its a Registered Retirement Savings Plan (RRSP) that has tax saving advantages because the income you earn is not taxed until it is withdrawn. OK. Noted. Not applicable right now. Something for the future perhaps?

It seems I need a T1 form. Do I have a T2 form? Ummm, a T3, a RC62, RC210, I need some form from my bank about my savings, there's something about not paying tax if you earn less than $10,000 and change and . . . oh give me a break. Seriously.

And so, I do the only thing I can do. I save the form, and decide I will go back to it later. Much, much later. Mañana always gets things done, right?

That much later comes just weeks before the deadline (well I am deadline driven). I decide I may as well just try and wing this. Give them as much information as I can that they want, afterall I have nothing to hide, and I am claiming nothing back. They seriously can't get me for not claiming for anything and basically saying "take my money" can they?

Not the wisest move I know, but right now, I am a tax return virgin, and I just want to get my first time out of the way. I fill out all the various boxes, we sign the forms, stick them in an envelope and wave them goodbye. Done. Yay, so proud of me.

(Sidenote: In Canada, income tax is administered by the Canada Revenue Agency (CRA). The Canadian income tax year is from January 1 to December 31. If you owe income tax, you must pay it by April 30 for the previous calendar year. If you are self-employed, the CRA gives you a bit longer to submit your income tax return. If you were employed or had an investment income your employer or financial institution will send you statements commonly referred to as "slips." These include T3 Statement of Trust Income Allocation and Designations, T4 Statement of Remuneration Paid, T5 Statement of Investment Income. Just keep everything on file! Online, look up Personal Income Tax on the Government of Canada website.)

***

Chapter 20

WHY DON'T EMPLOYERS GET BACK TO YOU?
(And yes, it's still April 2008)

It dawned on me today that people in Vancouver are not very good at getting back to you.

Since arriving here, Nathan and I must have applied for more than 100 jobs each.

Most applications are done online and at the end they say "please don't phone. You will hear from us if you are to be invited to an interview." So we thought that's probably the best thing to do. Until recently.

Before we arrived we had been warned that most jobs are through word of mouth or meeting people. Everyone will want to help you out, but as you know, it's not all that easy getting a friend a job, unless you are the boss.

So Nathan decided to test the theory the other day, and phone up one of the jobs he was keen on with a construction site. The woman, a very pleasant lady, told Nathan she had never received his email, and that considering his experience, he would have been suitable for a recent position right here in Vancouver. Unfortunately the position had gone to another less qualified person.

We decided to ignore the "don't call" note again, with a job at a local tourism site. After sending our resumes in as they'd requested, and not hearing anything, we decided to go to the local career fair and meet them in person.

The woman who represented the tourism firm was lovely, wrote down our names and asked us to come for an interview that weekend.

It all went well.

And then we heard nothing. So we phoned them up, and they said yes, we'd love you to come for another interview, how does this Tuesday suit you.

Just goes to show, don't always believe what they put on the internet, because a phonecall or two may just get you where you want to go.

We've got three weeks left until the end of the season.

Oh…my…gawd.

That means we really need to get a job. It's not that finding a job will be a problem. There's enough signs saying "help wanted" in all the local shops, the trouble is, we don't know what we want to do.

Part of us thinks it would be great to spend the summer in Vancouver. We are moving into our friends place just off the beach in Kitsilano in two weeks. The rent is minimal and Vancouver in the summer is meant to be better than the winter, so we have heard. But then again, we want to eventually end up in the Interior, don't we?

We've been looking at Nelson. An amazing old gold mining town that reminds us of Breckenridge in Colorado. It's quaint, everyone knows each other, property is cheap (an average family house costs $266,000) and it's the kind of place we can see ourselves settling down in.

To get a job, we'd need to live there. Do we up sticks at the end of the season and get a job, any job, and start building our life where we want to end up, or do we have a great summer here and see what happens?

It's not that we haven't got any choice, we've just got too many really and we don't know what we want. First World problems.

We didn't realize this would be our biggest problem when we arrived.

I've applied for a job in Nelson on a local newspaper. Perhaps I should follow up with a phone call, even though the application says not to...

Despite having applied for a variety of jobs, we've heard very little. Mind you, when we came out here we knew that applying through the normal route wouldn't get us very far.

With only a few weeks left until the end of the season, we've got to get our butts in gear. We've applied to Capilano Suspension Bridge, a top tourist attraction. Basically, we don't care what role we do as long as we aren't out of a job. That, however, hasn't got us anywhere.

Strangely enough, we walk past the YWCA and see an advert for a job fair. It's on our day off so we decide to pop down as the staff from Capilano will be there again.

There's a frenzy of people when we arrive. It's weird. I would have thought it would have been lots of teenagers, but the majority of people are 40-plus and it makes me worry a bit about the job situation.

We squeeze our way through the crowds, sign in, and head on over to the free coffee stand, of course.

After checking out the BC Ferries stand – oh my goodness, they pay over $20 an hour for ferrying cars onto the ships, now that is an option – we head to the Capilano Suspension Bridge team. After chatting to a lovely HR manager, it seems they never received our resumes. The trouble with the internet is that people think it speeds up the process, but when a company gets hundreds of applications for one post, chances are your email will get mislaid or be deleted, or the cloud will whip it off somewhere never to be seen again.

The HR manager tells us to come by for a group interview that weekend.

Oh goodness, I really am not a fan of interviews. I'd better get used to this.

I really hope at least one of us gets a job soon. This is crazy being in a new country and always being on the verge of something good. I suppose it is just the unknown, in just about everything we are doing right now.

So I'm sat in a room with four other people, and five people interviewing. When we're asked who has never been to a group interview, I raise my hand. I'm the only one! What's even more daunting is that I'm having a group interview with my husband. I feel like a right idiot. He's so good at interviews. I, however, am so used to interviewing others and not being in the spotlight, and I have the mindframe of "please give me the job, I'll prove I can do it well and guarantee you'll be happy."

The interview starts. We're asked to introduce ourselves...ooh I like this. This is like being at Brownie camp. Then come the questions. Explain a time when you had to take the lead? Can you tell us about a time when you had to control a crowd and deal with safety? Explain to us a time when something went wrong at work and what did you do? Tell me about a time when you received excellent customer service?

Ooh, I know this one. Nathan and I had discussed this very question a few days earlier. We were sitting on the couch when I said that I get stumped when they ask those kind of generic questions like the one about customer service. Nathan said to make it up if I can't think of something. Nope, I'm no good at that. So he says, "well think about the service we got from the bank when we arrived in Canada. How the lady sent us a Christmas card and all those little touches."

So I'm sitting here, thinking should I use that when Nathan raises his hand. Please don't use it, please don't use it. He doesn't. Bless his heart. I know what he's doing. His example isn't anywhere near as good as the one he gave me the other day, but he has done it on purpose as he can see I'm nervous.

So I raise my hand and give my example. It receives a great reception.

I realize I've got to get over my fear of sounding like I'm showing off when I give examples. I know I've been in a unique position, like many journalists, where I got to experience some crazy stuff. And just because I've been doing a job for the past 12 years that's given me the opportunity to say, join the Navy, become a rescue diver, join the fire brigade, race with the world class racing drivers (see, I feel like I am showing off, but it's all true), deal with the Mafia, doesn't mean I can't dig deep and use those experiences in interviews.

No, I must listen to my Canadian peers. As long as it's in the right context, it's not showing off, right? I just need to stand out. So I decide to use a few examples.

It goes so well that I'm asked to stay behind for a one-on-one interview for the position of Nature Guide. I think my award for environmental writer of the year helped with that.

It turns out to be a general chat about how I'd feel working in a rainforest and wearing a rangers uniform.

I leave the interview and give Nathan a hug. He's an angel.

We still haven't heard from Capilano Suspension Bridge, so we decide to phone them up. They say they are pleased we reminded them and they will get on the case. A few days later we still haven't heard, so we send an email. The next day, we are invited up for a third interview. I'm starting to understand the Canadian interviewing system now.

I'm back in the rainforest and being interviewed by another member of the Capilano staff. This time the interview is a lot more grueling. I actually feel really nervous. Why?

I'm interviewed by two girls. One playing good cop, the other bad cop. They ask those questions that stump me, like "we see you are and academic. Do you think you will try and overwhelm our visitors with your knowledge?" Oh how little they know!

I never knew that being knowledgeable about nature could be my downfall of being a nature guide. I get the impression one of the girls really likes me, but the other is, perhaps understandably, dubious.

So the interview goes up and down like a rollercoaster and every time my hands are in the air, I get that racing heart feeling again. That is, until, I decide to pull out the trump card. I'm asked how I've reacted in the past to safety issues. So I describe a few situations I've experienced on the mountain and then mention that I joined the fire service for a week and learned how to save people from burning buildings.

The atmosphere suddenly changes. "It takes a special something to join the fire service," says one of the girls. I kind of misread what they're saying and say "yes, I have total respect for them." Hang on a minute. Are they talking about me? Then the answers come flying. I can perform a guide in German if necessary. I speak a little Spanish. I've interviewed some of the world's top environmentalists. In England I'd feel like I was going too far, but they seem to be lapping it up. I leave feeling a little jaded. Why? I have no idea whether they like me or not.

Nathan's interview for maintenance went well. He got on famously with the chap.

The next day we get a phonecall. We've got the jobs! Yippee. I am a nature guide. Nathan is a maintenance man. Hilarious. I just love it. What a change. When would you ever get the chance of having such a diverse career change in your 30s in England? I send an email to my mum and dad.

They are even more excited than when I got into journalism. My dad tells me it was always his dream to do that kind of job, and could he help. I don't think they've ever been so proud. Hang on a minute. I'm only earning $12 an hour.

Mind you, that's the same as the snowboard instructor position and at least I will be working more than the guaranteed four hours a day. We will have so much money compared to what we've been used to. Perhaps we can buy a piece of fish to go with our rice? Cha-Ching!

(Sidenote: In Canada, the places to search for jobs today are indeed.com, workopolis.com, and monster.ca. The problem is, it seems the response rate is rather low. A great way to find out about vacancies is to get involved in networking groups, or hand deliver your resume to companies you want to work for. Also, asking to meet up for a coffee and a chat works great. Networking is essential in Canada.)

(Sidenote 2: Don't expect to hear back from companies after applying for a job. In Canada, unlike the UK, you rarely get a "you were unsuccessful" email. You will just receive radio silence. Also, don't be surprised if you get a call four months after you applied for a job.)

***

Chapter 21

TIME TO CHANGE THE WAY WE THINK

I've started reading *Secrets of the Millionaire Mind* by T. Harv Eker. It was given to Nathan by a property guy he met up with, who by the way never got in touch again. Weird.

It's an inspirational book that is actually better than it sounds. It says people tend to get stuck in a rut. If they have £3,000 in their savings, that's the kind of saving they will always have. If they come into money, they will somehow get rid of it and return to that same amount. The same happens if you're in debt. You'll always find yourself in debt by that amount, no matter how hard you try to get out of it.

That struck a chord with me.

The basic idea is that we grow up thinking a certain way about money. Me, I've discovered I repeat the adage "you only need enough to be comfortable. Money doesn't make you happy." The book says, if you're rich, you're comfortable. If you're comfortable, you're always on the edge – it's a never-ending cycle. What it does is make me reassess working for someone else. That way, I will never truly be in control of my money. Like, there is a maximum, no matter how hard I work.

This is something that has been niggling me for ages. Back in England, my best friend and I thought about starting up a cosmetic magazine. You know, capitalize on all the those offering enhancements. Think big, right? We'd looked into it and everything looked good. But then I was moving, so I didn't want to commit to something that I couldn't follow through with, so we put a halt to it.

I realized after doing that, that in fact it wouldn't be such a stupid idea. I edited a magazine for four years on my own, and Nathan has the sales skills, so would it really be such a stupid idea to just try and make a go of it?

After reading the new book, I realize I've got to take risks and to be honest, after looking around at the press and magazines in Vancouver, it wouldn't be too difficult to compete, would it?

So the thing is, we've come up with this idea to go to major companies who seem to have no idea how to market themselves, and offer to do everything from writing brochures or flyers to full blown magazines. That way they get a quality product and we don't have to dip into our savings too much.

The more we talk about it, the more sense it makes.

We can get the advertisers to pay for the publication, and then the cost to the client for whom we are making the magazine, is minimal. A win-win situation.

The trouble is, I start thinking about this in bed. Poor Nathan, because then I start chatting with him and neither of us can sleep. Should we just go for it? Afterall, it's the land of opportunity for us and from what we've experienced so far, people move to a slower beat here than in the UK.

So here I am, tip-tapping away creating an intro for our magazine. We've got the name of some printing companies, some rate cards from various magazines (oh my word they charge so much for advertisements here), now all we've got to do is make an appointment with the printers, come up with a company name and register ourselves an self-employed. Can it really be that easy? Let's throw caution to the wind. I have a millionaire mind and an entrepreneurial attitude. Watch me go!

Hang on a minute, we came for the simple life and we are slotting into our old life, no? Oh the irony.

(The very next day)

Nathan wants to trek down the Amazon.

Are you keeping up? I know, I know. This is the life we lead.

Let me fill you in. A friend of ours, a big burly chap from Aberdeen, is planning to spend seven months rafting single-handedly down the Amazon. If he completes it he will be the second person to have done this, ever.

He needs back-up. Someone on dry land to follow him in case he gets in trouble, and Nathan has offered his services.

We were sat chatting over coffee on Edgemont Village in North Vancouver, when I suddenly saw this look on Nathan's face. One of those looks where you think, oh goodness, what now?

Nathan then says, I've just offered to be the back-up support for the trip, don't you think that would be amazing. It's seven months.

Vancouver? Okanagan? Nelson? Now the Amazon?

Part of me gets really quite excited. What an adventure. I could write a book about the adventure perhaps?

Nathan is suddenly jumping on that idea thinking it could set us up for our chalet. I have to gently remind him that any money that could potentially come from that (if a publisher would even contemplate the idea) would end up being spent on the trip, because these kind of trips cost money.

I can see his face drop. A sudden realization that it wouldn't be as easy as getting in a car, following the Amazon while I tip-tap away on a laptop that has perfect internet connection. Because, yes, that would be exactly it.

I feel like part of me needs to grow up and say something. To pull in the reins a little. We have to focus on one thing at a time. The other part thinks, you've only got one life, don't be THAT wife.

I know if I commit to something I wouldn't want to let the person down. So if we say yes to the Amazon, we have to forget about setting up a new life in Canada for two years.

That's the reality...sadly.

Perhaps we just won't ever settle?

(Just two weeks later)

It's the end of the season.

You know what that means? No, not a trip to the Amazon! Nathan has gone quiet on that idea after I reminded him that we'd have to use our savings and when our Argentinian friend started laughing while pointing at me saying "Gringa, nooooo."

She then went on to explain, in her lovely broken English, that it's not the wild animals we have to be worried about, but the authorities. She says that its standard practice to get stopped and have to pay some kind of fee or something, but the nail in the coffin came when she pointed at me and said "with blond hair. Nooooo."

So as you can see, no Amazon trip.

Instead we are faced with the end-of-season party. A chance for staff to dress up and hit the mountain.

All the management have taken over looking after the lifts, so it's time for everyone else to celebrate. And for ski school that means one thing. Filling sprite bottles with vodka! Half the instructors are already pissed as farts. How on earth they are managing to ski and snowboard is beyond me? And Nathan looks like the Marlboro man in his check shirt and cowboy hat.

It's quite a quiet and relaxed day really, and for once, instead of pushing ourselves to the limit and hitting all the rails and jumps (and almost knocking a tooth out which I have been known to do on the last day), I decide to have fun and do a snowboard waltz down the slope with my Polish/Canadian friend. What a laugh.

I'm starting to realize that my worries about girlfriends are unfounded. My Polish friend in particular is such a gem and for some reason, since finding out she's a Scorpio (star sign, not insect silly) just like my mum, everything has made more sense. They are edgy, yet fiercely loyal. They also have that weird thing of being able to stare you in the eye whilst they talk to you and not blink. Honestly. Try it next time you find out a person is a Scorpio.

Although it's sad to wave goodbye to the end of the season, I'm excited about summer and most of our friends here are hanging around.

It's also time to say goodbye to the Nat that was hurt, pessimistic and childish (in the worst sense) and learn to trust again. Goodbye negativity, hello happy trusting thoughts. Could I be becoming "Canadian" already? Or maybe just finally growing up . . .

***

Chapter 22

WEATHER THE WEATHER
(April 18, 2008)

It's dumping with snow. Welcome to Canada!

***

Chapter 23

MY FIRST "REAL" JOB

We come home to a message on the answer machine. It's from the editor of Bunkerworld. He wants to see me. "Hi Natalie, we'd like to invite you for an interview this Friday at 2pm. If you could get back to me on…."

I have no idea who that is? What have I even applied for? But someone has got back to me!

You see I now get so excited when someone gets back to me because it's so rare. In the UK, from what I am used to, you apply for a job, and if you're not the right caliber, at least you'll get a stock standard letter saying they will keep your resume on file and you can move on.

In Vancouver, either they will get back to you three months after you've applied – and that's usually because the final date of application is two months after the advert has gone in the paper, even though the advert said, "person required immediately for busy team" – or, you never hear a thing. Unless you phone, which as I've said, they tell you not to do.

Somehow, just somehow, they still manage to get things working tickedy boo here.

I am also invited back for an interview as an editor of a food and wine magazine and been offered the potential of some freelance roles. But Bunkerworld, who could this be?

I get on the internet. It seems bunkering is the supply of fuel for ships. No way! What on earth? It can't be a magazine about that surely? After two-hours I realize that it is about shipping in general, ports and the environmental issues. I actually find it really interesting. Why is it that the position of editor for a food magazine, which I am eventually offered, ignites nothing in me, nada, but bunkering leaves me wanting more.

What a geek!

I've got the interview on Friday and I'm really excited. I suppose because for once I want to find out more. It's as much an interview about them as it is me. And being a journalist, I like that.

***

Chapter 24

BUILDING BUDDIES

I've taken the plunge. I've actually arranged to go out with my Polish friend on a "date." Gfffaw. We have the most amazing day.

Girls in Canada, well this one for sure, is awesome.

She was amazing fun. We tried on various hats, laughed about nothing in particular and chatted about everything. It was such a fun, easy-going day.

(Next day)

I'm bored. It's Saturday night. Nathan has fallen asleep on the sofa. This is the first time I can actually say I really wish we had some close friends here. Then we could pop around their house for a drink and pleasant conversation. Our new friends are all in Whistler for the week. Anyway, you feel a bit awkward just phoning them up at the last minute and saying "what are you up to?" That takes time to get to that stage.

I do miss that easy relationship you have with old friends.

Nathan suddenly wakes up. We decide to pop to Starbucks for a coffee. As we sit in the window watching the world whizz by, reading the papers, I realize that although I miss my friends and family, I am very lucky to be here with him.

***

Chapter 25

BEAUTIFUL, BOUNTIFUL BERYL

I've received an email from Beryl.

Let me tell you a little bit about Beryl. We met when I was moving back to England from Spain. She was sitting next to me on the plane. A kind and gentle lady in her early 70s. We started chatting, as you do, and it turned out she was a freelance journalist. The stories she came up with made me blush…and that's saying something.

For that two hour flight I was entertained. I discovered she lived in the south of Spain. Her children live in England and they think she is mad for having just left on her own. For some reason, we just clicked. So we exchanged emails.

That's not something I normally do, or if I would, I'd never consider keeping in touch, but Beryl was different.

This was her first email:

Hello Sunshine - trust all is well, and that you have had lots of new experiences since we met (plane).

This wee machine apparently had a touch of flu, so did not get lots of e.mails the past month.

Keep smiling - and in touch - visit sometime, beryl

Her next email after I wished her a Happy New Year:

Yep. Keeping warm. Happy New Year sunshine........chilly winds here at times, but you know about those.............looking after two dogs for friends, ow, in nightie and fur hat first thing in morning, will make News of the World yet!

Visit any time,,,,,love beryl, oh, either me or one of the dogs bit through cable, so was without line for several days, just in case any reply to e.mails seem rather rudely delayed.

Then came this one:

Oh scrumptiousness - Just met someone from North East Spain, and we are planning lots of well, journeying shall we say...if it is anything like the last, well, Spanish.

I arrived at bus stop only 24hrs early.....then, six next morning was woken by an irate coach driver 'where are you'..well, and I had just rescued two friends, wrong dates of course, not my fault might add. Its me lifestile....mad dash to Alicante, half-dressed and only half packed.

Took a swim suit and sandals! Need I go on, all giggles but the Spanish lot no sense of fun at that stage....14 hrs my dear, three pit stops and me worn out already.

Hotel decor was dia, dia or, oh hell, shit coloured swirls.......but staff great.

Others went on outings, I elected to do my own thing........oh glorious.

Walked in meadows massed with wild flowers, inc., orchids..........the cows wore bells, I was transported. And of course it rained. Oh bliss.

Trains were wild. Had internal massages along the route.....not bad for a couple of euros..........and so it continued. Learned a lot, loved it all, and had a bad stomach at the end and had two injections in my bum. All in a good cause I say.

Bought me a snorkle (sic) today, wonder if the lungs will hold out. Oh well, I shall die trying tra la.

Long life and happiness darling girl, keep your pendulum centered.........

beryl xxxx

You get the idea. Beryl is one of those people you rarely come across. A vibrant spirit. Someone you hope to be when you are older.

For some reason she has been on my mind and I decide to update her. It must have been a year since we were last in touch. That's four years since we first met on the flight home.

It turns out Beryl is now what she calls retired.

Well she's 76, and has been getting lost in Valencia, and being picked up by the police. Wow, she's amazing. She tells me that as I've moved to Canada she is now feeling the warm breeze of Spain and the cool breeze of Canada.

There's something so comforting about emailing Beryl.

Knowing she's getting into all sorts of mischief and still living it up at 76 makes me feel the warm and fuzzies.

I wonder if I will hear back?

*** ***

Chapter 26

FATHER/SON BATTLE – SISTER/SISTER LOVE

Nathan's dad hasn't replied to an email he sent him.

After we returned from Austria, Nathan decided to put his thoughts into a letter and send them to his dad. It was very honest. It sums up all the pent up anger he has. Nathan's letter is pretty open. He basically says he's worried about his dad and that he won't be there for the wedding because of this. You get the gist.

Do I agree? Hey, it's his family, it's his choice, right, and I can only advise and support him.

But it's such a tough one for him. I can see that. How do you deal with it when you believe in your heart they aren't happy?

Three weeks on and Nathan gets an email, asking him if he will be coming to the wedding, so Nathan responds asking if he received his letter? No reply. Communication isn't a strong point for some I suppose. It's hard to know what to do here. I so want to try and bring them together, but interfere, and I could end up making things worse.

All I can do is try and help repair the relationship if its goes tits up.

My sister has come to stay, for a whopping 24 hours! Crazy, right? But that's the life of cabin crew.

I'm so excited. Here I am skipping around the house after listening to a message from my sister saying she has flown in to Seattle and will be catching the bus up to see us for 24 hours. I am going to be sick with excitement! I can hardly sleep.

The next day we race down to the bus station. Every bus that comes, I run up to see if it's her. After about 10 minutes I see her little blond hair and smiley face. Can life get any better?

We take her back to the house we are now staying in now, in Kitsilano (remember that Hank I mentioned who shipped our CDs to Vancouver? Well he has gone back to the UK for a few months and asked us to look after his place). Lucky ducks, us that is. My sis and I take a walk along the beach to Granville market. Nothing changes, we chat as if we saw each other yesterday.

We watch the boats coming in, we laugh, we eat half a pita (or "peter" as they say in Canada) and I point out all the great things about being here. I'm really trying to sell this place it seems – for some reason I want her to love it as much as I do and see why I moved (it seems to be an expat thing to do when we move. Like we need to justify why we are here).

After a jaunt into downtown Vancouver, we head to the diner for food.

Time goes by so quickly, but it just feels so right having her here. Before we know it, it's 10pm and the poor soul has jet-lag, but she's keeping it together so well. So we wish each other good night, climb into bed and drift off to sleep. I am so happy. I wake up early the next morning because I want to spend as much time with her as possible before she goes home.

My parents brought us up with the attitude that you should spend every minute like it is your last. That's great in some ways, as you end up appreciating people more. In other ways all you can think of is, "what if this is the last time I see this person?" Which inevitably ends up with us crying.

So there we are, standing at the bus stop crying like two big babies. Yes, I vowed not to cry, but saying goodbye just gets harder. I wave her off, with Nathan holding my hand. I have the biggest lump in my throat.

For the rest of the day I'm like a child who has had her favourite toy taken away. If I could stamp my feet and have a tantrum right now, I probably would.

That's what you have to put up with when you move away from family. I'm so lucky my sister has a job that brings her here.

She phones me a few days later and says when she told the crew about us saying goodbye, she had them in tears too!

***

Chapter 27

CAPILANO SUSPENSION BRIDGE
(May 2008)

Nathan and I have just attended our five-hour safety training for our job with Capilano Suspension Bridge.

I feel a bit bad as there is the potential of that other job, but as my mother always said, marry rich, oh no hang on, wrong one, she said you've got to keep your options open.

Nathan has already started his job as maintenance man at Capilano and he is really enjoying it. I've never seen him this relaxed, but he says he also feels like he isn't using the skills he has. It's a bit of a mind conflict right now. The trouble is, it's a great job, and seriously, working outside, drinking coffee, firing beer barrels to make them into plant pots and so on is stress free and quite rewarding, but he says he wants to get back into property consultancy again, which is what he did before we left the UK.

He, like me I've gathered, defines himself through his job. It's a very British trait I gather. In Canada, if you work in a restaurant, it's great because it's a good job often with great medical benefits. You don't get judged from what I see.

We still haven't quite adapted to that way of thinking yet.

The five hours of safety training for me, which starts off at 4pm, is rather, how can I put this, long-winded, as most meetings are. We are surrounded by kids. Gosh, I feel like my parents. These "kids" are actually teenagers, but compared to Nathan and I, they are little sprogs.

I see that there's definitely potential here to progress through the ranks if you can just stick with the low pay for a while and prove yourself, which is fair.

The first hour is an introduction to the rainforest. Quite handy considering at Grouse we missed our orientation, and I can tell you, on foggy days when you can't see your hand in front of your face, I thanked my lucky stars that I had a map of the slopes imprinted on my brain.

The second hour, we take a tour of the rainforest. It's quite remarkable really. To have a 62-million acre rainforest right on your doorstep. The area is about so much more than the bridge that stands 240 feet off the ground and is wide enough that you can get two 747 jumbo jets, tip by tip, side by side in the canyon (can you tell the information is sinking in).

I, like other people, had originally thought the entrance price a little steep, but when you realize how much work goes into it, it all make sense. Ooh, I can feel myself getting on brand already.

Nathan and I hang back from the group and start playing around. We're like kids. We push and shove each other and giggle like teenagers. Why is it that the older you get, the more fun it is to monkey around?

The next two hours are rather grueling. We have to perform role plays, to show we can use the walkie talkies. I don't like role plays. Drama at school was never my thing, but hey ho, gotta be a team player.

Then we're taught how to exceed in customer service.

By 8pm I'm starting to drift off. Is it just me, or when you get tired do you start to feel like a naughty child and get a bit insolent, not wanting to answer those obvious questions, and start playing with your clicky pen, or snapping your ruler?

All in all, it's great they have these training days, but sometimes, I just get the feeling that they could cut them short and it would sink in better. This ain't no TED talk.

We walk out of the beautiful rainforest, soak in the nature around us and mull over the reason why we moved, and climb into our gas guzzling 4x4.

Interview day. Which one? You think you're having a bad time keeping up, trust me, my life feels like a whirlwind right now.

It's the interview with Bunkerworld, you know, the shipping fuel thingamajig.

I get the bus downtown and end up at an office on the Waterfront. I've made some notes, and I'm stood outside the office block reading them when this guy comes up to me with a coffee in his hand, and in a perfect English accent says "Natalie?" You can tell he's English, because he doesn't say "Nadalee?"

"Hi, I'm Martin from Bunkerworld. I gathered it was you as you were clutching those notes." How embarrassing. Oh well. We have a good old chat in the elevator about the location of the office. It may sound strange, but I can already see myself working here. Maybe it is because it's like a taste of home?

We walk into the office and Guy, a New Zealander, stands up to greet me. It turns out there is just the two of them, but that the company is global and in fact the leading company of its kind in the world. I'm liking this already.

Martin is a right laugh. He keeps cracking jokes and it turns out that both he and Guy also knew nothing about bunkering before they started either.

I'm in with a chance.

For once, I'm not faltering when they ask questions, because I seem to have the answers. In fact it seems the way they run the company is very similar to my last company. Guy plays the bad cop, or as best he can because he is a really nice guy.

I get asked standard questions, like how I would deal with a situation when the story is about one of our major advertising clients . . . easy, don't upset the bill payers, but still get the story out there, and various other similar questions.

Martin intervenes every now and then, asking how I will handle being back in an office after working outdoors. He knows the answer, but I still give it, saying I've worked in an office for 12 years, it won't come as a shock.

Then comes the question of working in an office with just the three of us. All I can envision is peace and quiet. Coming from a busy editorial office where phones are constantly ringing, and you have to build up an ability to switch off during a telephone interview and just listen to the voice at the end of the phone, the idea of being in a peaceful office is lovely.

Then they tell me the hours. Monday to Friday, 8am to 4.30pm. Come again? Did I hear correctly?

Wow. When I first got into journalism I was told the hours are long and when you're not working, you still are. That's so true. I could never go to a function without leaving with a story and ending up with someone's phone number to get an interview, or spending the entire evening advising people how to get free publicity.

8am to 4.30pm. Wow.

Then comes the second layer of icing on the cake. "We'd expect two stories a day." Two? Just two? I never thought I could come to Canada, continue with my love of writing, and write about something so interesting, and get quality of life to boot. I want this job!

When I say I wouldn't want any less than $45,000 a year, they don't flinch. Shoot, I should have said more. Almost an hour later and the interview is over. I offer to leave my references, but they shift a little awkwardly, and say if I get through to the next interview they will take a look.

I have this weird feeling now.

It all seemed to go so well, but they didn't want my references. They nodded at all the right points, and smiled as if I was saying all the right things, but they just said "if" I get through to the next interview.

I can't wait for the day when I no longer need to go for another interview and I can just do my work and see a fairly decent pay cheque every two weeks.

I go home to a grubby looking Nathan who's been pitching tents all day; the canopy kind, and tell him about it. He seems even more excited than me.

I guess if one of us gets a better paying job, then it takes the pressure off the other one.

That evening Nathan sits at the computer looking at houses and what we could afford with me on my wage and Nathan on his. It seems a lot. There's a gorgeous looking three bedroom house with a garden and everything in our price range.

His eyes have lit up. He's already living there, with a spaniel and a golden doodle running around the yard.

It's my first "shadow day" at Capilano Suspension Bridge. You keeping up? I don't blame you if not, what a whirlwind.

It's the first time I've driven alone. I'm in a city, on the wrong side of the road (well the right side, but you know what I mean, otherwise that would mean I'd have crashed by now), in a massive car! Ahhhhhhh!

I seem to be doing rather well until I get to a junction where the light has gone red, but I'm allowed to turn right anyway, and as I'm about to put my foot on the accelerator a Porsche screeches past, so I put the brakes on, and find I'm stopped on the pedestrian crossing area.

Believe me when I say the pedestrian is king out here. Next thing I see an angry face looking into the car as I've blocked his way for a few seconds. I mouth "sorry" which startles him, and drive on.

You live and learn.

Remember, most lights you can turn right on red, but pedestrians will be crossing too.

I learn on that first day at Capilano that there are three native trees to our rainforest, the Douglas fir, the western hemlock and the red cedar. I learn that the First Nations (don't dare call them Indians or native Americans as I learned from a lovely First Nation guy called Peter) consider the cedar the tree of life, and all the things they use the trees for.

I learn and learn. I feel like I'm going to end up being David Attenborough. I'm like a sponge. I get into journalist mode, and keep asking questions. I must be so annoying.

What an amazing place to work. Even if it is for $12 an hour.

Hang on, what was that. We are open until 10pm in the summer? Oh yea, tourism.

So here I am, in a job that gets you outdoors and is a wonderful opportunity, and yet the hours mean that you don't have a quality of life outside of work. This makes no sense. What to do, what to do.

The people who work here are so happy however. Where else would you get to hear over the radio that a bear is in the area and to be aware, or see a bald eagle swoop down into the canyon and catch a salmon. Or see a cheeky osprey or otter dive into a pond and catch a fish?

Then again, it's a tourist attraction. You get all the tourists, so there's camera flashes going off everywhere, and despite being on holiday, some people can get rather tetchy. And the hours, oh the hours.

Am I talking myself out of this because I know it's an opportunity of a lifetime, and yet part of me wants to get back into an office where I can shut myself off from people if I want?

I finish at 6.30pm after a nine hour day, put on CFox, my favourite rock radio station, and blast on down the road in my 4x4 back across the bridge, into downtown and off to the beaches.

Yes. This really is the life.

Chapter 28

FIRST NATION ENLIGHTENMENT

This is turning out to be so interesting. At Capilano Suspension Bridge I work with a lot of First Nation folk who are fantastic and so knowledgeable. It seems, after speaking to Peter who is Squamish Nation, that although there is trouble with drink and drugs within some First Nation communities, like most of society, they are trying to teach the younger generation their history and often struggle to keep it and their languages alive.

I delve deeper and get the feeling that yes, of course they are upset about the land being taken from them, and that yes, the Europeans are to blame for bringing diseases over and claiming the land as their own, when all the First Nation people did was offer them shelter, clothing and medicine to get rid of scurvy by drinking Cedar tea (I joke with Peter that I bet he wished they hadn't done that now. Fortunately it goes down well and he laughs).

I get the impression however that the Brits are the ones they are more, should I say, aggrieved by. But from what I am gathering, Peter is more annoyed that the British tend to point the finger at others and forget about the atrocities that they've done in the past, which includes the cruelty the Native kids underwent at residential schools (if you don't know about that, I highly recommend you look it up).

I then tell him that yes, growing up as part German, I had experienced the finger pointing, and yet while I understood, many Brits also failed to acknowledge the atrocities carried out by the British Empire. Now, don't get me wrong, I'm not anti-brit, but I think those who point fingers should look at themselves first, no matter your race, age or history. Glass houses and stones, and all that.

So then I joke that I am of the Attila the Hun heritage anyway, as it has been proven the genes are strong across Europe and you just need to look at my family's facial features.

Well, all of a sudden, Peter becomes friendly. I have broken down the wall. He tells me the story of how an English woman was so distraught with his tales of how the British acted when they arrived in North America that when she asked how she could make it up to them, he said "just educate people." Then he tells me about the rituals of the Squamish Nation, and the ones that outsiders are or will never be invited to, and how his family have always lived in the area and lived off the land, and still do.

I am in awe. It's only when you get to speak to the First Nation people face-to-face, and take the time to understand their point of view that you get a real sense of the battles within Canada and how they are trying to move forward together with reconciliation and the current way of life, without losing who they are.

Before I landed in Canada, I had quite a romanticized view I suppose as you don't really get to experience the realities living in the UK, so it is great to be educated.

I feel well and truly enlightened. Thank you Peter.

(Sidenote: Interesting fact. Today, there are approximately 200,000 Indigenous people in British Columbia and 198 distinct First Nations in B.C.)

***

Chapter 29

JOBS COME OUT OF THE WOODWORK

For some time Nathan has been in contact with a guy who owns the local super car dealership. He doesn't really want to get back into car sales, but then again, he got on so well with the owner when he went to see him that he might consider it.

It seems the owner has been in England trying to sort something out that could possibly involve Nathan. And so he gets all excited, but we have to be realistic. Over here, when someone tells you they have got some great plans that involve you, it usually means they've started baking and would like you to try their cherry pie.

So Nathan goes to lunch with the owner and it turns out he was hoping to get another super car franchise and to get Nathan working on that. But it didn't happen.

He tells Nathan he would love him to work for him, but has no positions currently, but to keep in touch.

Nathan, bless him, is slightly despondent.

He knows he shouldn't be as I've got a good feeling and he is amazing at what he does, but he was hoping to get offered a job. His focus has gone from property to entering back into car sales, which he is great at. Flip-flopping back and forth, us? Never.

Patience, we know, we know…

I get a phonecall from Guy at Bunkerworld.

It seems I made an impression, and now it's between me and another person for who gets the job. I've made it to the final interview stage!

They want me to do a writing exercise to see what I can do.

It's like being back at school, but you kind of get used to it when you're a journalist. Clippings are never enough. I suppose the hand of an editor can have a lot to do with how an article turns out.

So I cancel my next "date" with my lovely Polish friend to dedicate time to writing the story. She is super cool about it.

The story is about the ports of LA and Long Beach and their incentive plan to encourage low sulphur emissions. You may find it rather dull. Me, being a mega-nerd, I find it uber interesting. (Oh the realities of writing in the business world.)

I contact the ports to get the latest information and conduct short interviews, telling them what I am doing. They are super helpful. I have to go that extra (nautical) mile if I want this job.

A story that would usually take two hours at the most because I'm getting used to the style and the subject, actually takes me six hours. How? I have no idea! I just keep going over and over it again! I must really want this job.

I press the send button on Thursday evening at 10pm. It's gone, half a day before they wanted it. That's it. I've done my best. Fingers crossed.

***

Chapter 30

BACK HOME, BUT WHERE IS HOME?

I've just heard from my friends that England is starting to feel the impacts of the recession. I've got mixed feelings. People are being made redundant in the UK. At Nathan's old work people are being let go. House prices are starting to drop. There's even rumours that food prices are going to rocket. It's awful.

I'm sad for those it is affecting, and thankful we got out at the right time. Nathan could well have been out of work, and me, being in publishing, well, who knows.

I've just received a Facebook request from a former interviewee/friend called Richard.

Let me explain who Richard is. He's a clairvoyant. He's great. He read the cards of everyone from Princess Diana (and yes he said he did know she was going to die, but that unless you ask, he can't tell you) to Gregory Peck.

I met him through a friend and wrote a story about him. We got on like a house on fire.

Here's the interview that was published in the local Daily Echo newspaper on December 11, 2006, a year before we moved to Canada:

When people meet Dorset tarot grandmaster Richard de Meath for the first time, and find out that he read the cards for Princess Diana they ask the same question; did he see her death?

He rolls his eyes and simply answers, yes.

Richards says: "I told her I see a death in the family. She assumed it would be one of the older members. Why didn't I tell her? There's an unspoken rule in tarot reading, if you see something like that, you don't disclose it unless you are asked."

Needless to say, despite being slightly skeptical about tarot predictions, I will make sure I don't make the same mistake.

Richard is a character.

He's larger than life and has read the cards for royalty and celebrities including the Princess of Monaco, Elizabeth Taylor, Princess Diana, twice, and Vincent Price.

But there's so much more to this colourful man.

Richard will tell you he was born with a silver spoon in his mouth.

He was born in Athlone, Ireland, in 1944, went to Trinity College and ended up studying a Phd in Philosophy in Buffalo, USA.

He returned to London in the 1960s, where opportunities fell in his lap.

He became a model, a very unusual and profitable profession for a man back then, and he lived for many years in Paris and Milan.

Richard says: "Modelling opened the door to acting. I was asked to appear in everything from a hairdresser in Sunday Bloody Sunday, starring Glenda Jackson, to Carry on Camping.

It was during filming in 1971 that he met Elizabeth Taylor.

"She discovered I read tarot and asked if I could read for her, in front of her entire family. No, I'm not at liberty to disclose what was said, but I can tell you she wasn't a diva."

During his acting career he also met Vincent Price on the set of The Revenge of Dr Death.

Richard explains: "He had the most fascinating hand, very lined. He was an old soul.

"It was a difficult reading. I'd read an article on him a week before, but everything I saw was the opposite. That's the first time I've doubted my abilities.

"I was embarrassed telling him, but it turned out I was right."

You could spend hours listening to Richard talk about his experiences and encounters with the rich and famous, but for Richard tarot card reading is all about helping people out in their time of need.

He says people will turn to tarot as a last resort, which means he has to be very careful. But he says tarot isn't the hocus pocus it's made out to be.

Richard says: "Tarot card reading is like reading hieroglyphics. 100 years ago people couldn't understand them. Then they found a way of translating the messages.

"Unfortunately there are a lot of frauds out there and that can be dangerous."

Having the gift however doesn't mean Richard has had an easy life. Far from it. He's gone from being a millionaire in the 1960s to squandering it all.

Richard says: "I've definitely had a roller coaster of a journey. I've lived many lives in this one and I've

*finally ended up in Winterbourne Kingston, where
I'm finally happy!"*

My cards
*I'm not too keen on tarot reading, I believe what
will be will be, but Richard has built my trust up so
I decide to have my cards read and here is what
they say, in brief anyway.*

Past lives
*Richard shocks me by telling me I don't want
children, which is true and I haven't told him
anything yet! He says it's because I died in a past
life during childbirth. Freaky!*

Past (this life)
*Richard tells me I have travelled a lot and lived in
many places over the past seven years, which is
true. He says a friendship at 13 made me
mistrusting, but that it's a good way of protecting
myself. Again very true.*

Present
*Strangely enough my husband Nathan is strong in
this reading, and Richard jokes that he is hogging
the limelight. Richard says that six years ago there
was a death which has been central to our lives but
that we are coming out the other end, and that
things are starting to look very positive, especially
where money is concerned. The first part is true and
I'm keeping my fingers crossed for the second. He
also says a letter of an opportunity will come up on
Wednesday, which turns out to be true. Strange.*

Future
This is the kind of hand you want to be dealt.

Richard tells me news my husband and I have been waiting for is coming. He tells me monetary rewards are coming my way, and that doors are now opening.

He says although I will live a long life I must grab opportunities today. He says I will live a life richer than Brad Pitt and Angelina Jolie, and not in the monetary sense. And says, "oh love, you are in for a fantastic future." If anything, this gives me a kick I need.

Overall verdict
Although a lot of it could apply to anyone, there are quite a few times I am taken aback by how accurate Richard is with past events and times. It was fun, a bit strange at times, but it gives me a different view of my future, which is always good.

Strangely enough, it wasn't long after that we received news about being accepted into Canada.

So skip forward to now and Richard is in touch with me and his first question is, "How's the book going?"

I never mentioned I was writing a book...

***

Chapter 31

JOB SECURITY

I've got the job? I've got the job!

The one with Bunkerworld. I am so excited. It's all very well living the free and easy lifestyle, but the idea of actually being kept busy eight hours a day and having a weekend to look forward to and some money in the bank to eat a full meal is really quite exciting. Maybe it's the familiarity for now and stability?

It has been seven months since I had an office job, and I can't wait. I know after a few months I will crave being back in the great outdoors, but isn't it always the case that you want what you can't have? Maybe I just want some familiarity too? But baby steps to mega change, right?

I start next month.

Oh no, I'm going to have to tell Capilano that I have another job. And they've been so good to me. I hate this bit. I feel awful as they've put so much into the training and been so kind with me. But the interview was during training.

I feel like a right jerk.

The plus side. I won't have to work until 10pm or get attacked by mosquitoes, but I will miss my colleagues and the outdoors. There is something about nature people.

So I did the right thing. I've phoned Capilano to let them know, telling them it is an opportunity I can't really miss out on. I have this niggling thought in my head that if I stuck it out, then I could have worked my way up at Capilano, but in reality I know there are people that have been there a long time and would be the first in line for a promotion, and I am definitely not one to step on toes.

I've been asked to work for another week, which is fine. My first day back in after telling them is, to say the least, slightly awkward. I hang around a bit to chat to my direct supervisor, but she's on the phone and then turns to someone else who has just walked in to ask them how they are.

I'm not sure if she's blanking me or not. I suppose she'd have every right to if she was, so I'm not really miffed. Instead I decide it can wait, I grab a walkie-talkie and make my way across the bridge to head into the tree-house. Before I do, I take a quick detour around the pond. All of a sudden, out of nowhere, an Osprey, the size of a bald eagle, swoops down in front of me, talons outstretched and plunges into the pond, grabbing a fish. One slight pause and he (she? I can't tell the difference yet. Still a long way to go until I am David Attenborough it seems) is off again, through the trees, and off into the distance.

Wow. I mean how often do you get to see things like this while at work? In Canada it seems at least once a week! Stunning. As I walk past the skunk cabbage (yes it does smell of skunk), past the banana slugs (yes they do look like bananas) and past the resident Great Blue Heron (yes he's great and blue . . . Canada makes things so simple to remember in so many ways), I guess I start to wonder if I've been a bit hasty in taking the job.

Unfortunately life isn't that easy when you feel the pressure of money and supporting two people, and are trying to get a mortgage in a new land and in one of the most expensive cities in Canada – but I can dream.

An hour later, I get a call over the radio from first aid saying there's a woman coming across the bridge who is very scared and may need assistance at the other end.

Now considering the bridge is 450-feet high, and swings, I can understand some people getting nervous, but when I see this poor woman, whose name I soon find out is Gina, I can see this has been a massive ordeal for her.

She is frozen in terror. I start to chat to her about all the lovely things she will get to see on the other side of the bridge, all the wildlife, the trees and plants, and get her to look at me, and up to the trees as I guide her across.

At the other side I take her to a seat, give her a glass of water and inform first aid it's all OK. Then I run off to get her some fish food, so she can feed the rainbow trout and watch the frenzy.

She seems more settled, but I tell her to radio for me if she needs help.

It turns out that wherever I am, so is Gina, so I take her on a tree top tour, explaining to her all the wonderful things to look out for in a temperate rainforest (thanks Peter), and when it comes to crossing the big bridge again, it just so happens that

I'm heading back across for my lunch. So we walk together and eventually make it over.

As I wave her goodbye, and tell her not to worry about what anyone else thinks and that she conquered a massive fear today, she seems happy.

What follows?

The loveliest letter anyone could ever image. One sent to me via email and another to my boss.

It went on for two pages, saying how I'd been like a comfort blanket to her that day and that I went above and beyond.

That letter was so special in so many ways. Firstly because knowing I had touched someone's life was wonderful, but also because I was leaving, and it kind of showed my boss that it hadn't been a waste of time hiring me. Honest.

For the first time, I actually understood what a reward working in the service industry is.

It's not enough for me to say goodbye to better pay, but it makes up for an awful lot.

Incidentally, my boss tells me how much I will be missed.

I've heard back from another job. In fact since accepting the job at Bunkerworld I've heard back from quite a few. Like buses I tell ya.

And just like nature, Canadians tend to wake up in spring, and jobs that I applied for in January are now being offered to me. To be honest, I'm not bothered about any of them really. I'm going to be working great hours, with great people, doing something I enjoy for pay I am happy with.

So I dutifully respond, saying I now have another job, but thank you.

That is, aside from one job that Nathan is particularly keen on for me. Some months ago Nathan saw an advert in the Georgia Strait newspaper asking for a marketing/tourism manager to promote an area in the North Thompson Valley called Clearwater.

The ad went along the lines of: "Looking for somewhere that you can still buy cheap as chips housing in a small but expanding community, with not much here except nature?" Of course it wasn't quite like that, it was far more Canadian, but you get the idea.

Nathan told me I should apply. I really couldn't be bothered; I mean what marketing experience do I have to start with? But, as I said at the wedding, I will do, or something like that, and so I send off my resume and think nothing more of it . . . until I get an email saying they are interested.

Well blow me. I start to get nervous. Nathan seems so excited and starts looking at property prices in Clearwater (which start at around $100,000)! I start panicking about living in the middle of nowhere, but then I could live in our own house, with a yard, and have a dog that I could take to work. It all sounds like a Mills & Boon novel. Realistically though, I'm not so sure there would be a happily ever after.

Nathan, however, has already moved in, is mowing the lawn, going on mountain bike treks and taking the dogs on long jaunts to fend off the bears.

I bring him back down to earth and say, let's play it by ear. And guess what, I'm invited to attend an interview. What to do, what to do indeed?

Time for a road trip to Clearwater. The idea of a roadtrip is exciting and I start thinking, maybe we could make this work. Afterall, our big dream was to be in a remote area and live the simple life.

I start to feel like I've eaten too many E numbers, and I can tell you, I react off sugar and artificial colouring like a child. In fact, worse than a child.

Once I was tested for diabetes and my doctor sent me straight to the hospital. This was after he'd taken a reading and my blood sugar level was sky high. I then asked him if it made a difference that I had just eaten a whole bag of gummy bears? He calmed down and smiled, but said we should get it checked anyway.

Needless to say, I was fine, but it definitely got me thinking after I sat next to a gentleman with one leg in the diabetes ward who said he used to eat sweets like me.

Sorry, I digress. So yes. It's over 500 kilometres to Clearwater, so we decide to stop off at a place called Kamloops, the nearest big town, to see what civilization is like in that area.

The drive is stunning. It's raining on the way, but that doesn't make much difference. On the drive I see a black bear with her cub down by the side of the road, and an eagle swoops down over the hood (get me going all Canadian) of our car.

The journey seems really straight forward, but I see what they mean about the roads here. Because everything is long and straight, the roads that is, a four-hour journey seems like nothing. I mean you're not even halfway across BC in four hours. That would get you across half of England if there wasn't all that traffic. Things become relative when you're living in a province (not a state, don't get that wrong out here) that is almost seven times the size of England.

When we eventually arrive in Kamloops it's 2pm and it honestly just looks like a town that's been plonked in the middle of nowhere to serve one purpose, to give those who live there a sense of civilization. Which I suppose is what it says on the tin.

I'm still upbeat however. This would be our destination for say, furniture. Clearwater is where it's at.

When we arrive in Clearwater, we're not quite sure if we've arrived. It's so spread out. There's a section where you have a grocery store, a barbers and a dollar store, but then everything else is just scattered hither and thither.

Don't get me wrong. Clearwater is stunning. It's green, has the most impressive waterfalls, and is tucked away in nature's own pocket. Could I live here? No. I would go mad. No wonder people have got into wood carving here. Being remote in Canada is very, very different to being remote in the UK. We were quite naive about that before we arrived. Life lesson number 12345.

We stay on the outskirts in a place called Birch Island with a lovely couple called Linda and Jan (Yan) at the Windmill B&B. They are very welcoming and it so happens that they are selling their business – a five-bedroom B&B for just under $400,000. They talk about how they got married on January 4th (my birthday) and show us all their amazing woodwork, and I start to think, maybe this is fate. Maybe we should be living here, owning a B&B with dogs in the garden and Nathan mountain biking. There I go, flip flopping again.

But then I close that chapter of the romance novel to look at things a little more realistically. I would get bored shitless here. I'm in my 30s, not about to retire, and although we could easily just plod on for the rest of our lives, with a small mortgage, building up a business in a town that will undoubtedly grow one day….Nope, I can't do it, I just can't. Remote when you come from the UK, is very different to remote in Canada, that's for sure, especially when you're snowed in during the winter.

Fortunately, Nathan feels the same.

So we head out to dinner by the lake, which is stunning, and say how we will have to come back one day for a weekend break.

I've still got my interview tomorrow though, and although I now have no interest, we've come all this way, I may as well show up. Although I can tell you, it's so tempting to be like a kid and just not.

Suddenly, Nathan has a brainwave. That tends to happen to us quite a bit out here. He suggests heading down to Kelowna. It's all we've ever talked about since we first applied to move to Canada. We wanted to eventually move to the Okanagan, because you can get a lot more for your money and it's meant to be stunning. So it's about time we actually see it in the flesh. Funny how you can have ideas about a place without even seeing it.

We consider making a trip to Revelstoke as well, a place that has been coined the next Whistler, but decide to leave that for another day.

We're off to Kelowna, I've just got to get the interview out of the way first.

The interview goes well. Too well in fact. Why does that always happen? You shine in interviews where you don't want the job, coming up with great answers to their objectives and giving all the right nods in all the rights places. But heaven forbid should it be a job you really want, then you interrupt at the wrong time, nod when they ask "do you ever pull sickies," and just generally make a real tool of yourself.

The interview is held in the tourism office, which consists of a slightly more mature demographic shall we say, and a woman from Calgary who is desperately trying to train a team on how to use a very simple computer system.

I would die inside if I had to be here. Tick. Tock. Tick. Tock.

After 90-lonnnnng minutes we're off to Kelowna. We change in the car as temperatures have now reached 30 degrees Celsius and we drive through the pine beetle ridden valleys, up past the destructive forest fires of 2003 and then, like a vision, the land turns green again and before us lies the most magnificent lake I've ever seen in my entire life. It's breathtaking.

Welcome to Kelowna.

So, is Kelowna everything we thought it would be? Too right. It's like Tuscany.

Surrounded by wineries, secret beaches, and signs that say "a bear has been spotted here recently." It's to-die for.

Everything is so serene, apart from the boy racers who are driving around in their jacked up 4x4s with music blasting and their caps on backwards, and the groups of teens shouting f*** you b****. It's a bit like being back in Bournemouth on Westover Road.

That's the trouble with small towns.

There's a small town attitude no matter where you go in the world.

They want to be like the big city, and think in a way that they believe big cities think, but are just missing a key ingredient: they are not the big city.

Saying that though, that was just the "yoof" and no matter how much I like to try and believe I can pass as one, I'm not. It has been proven to me time and again as I question, "why would anyone wear their jeans under their bum?" But then, I'm sure the generation before mine wondered why my generation always had to have their G-string on show and get that muffin top when you bend down.

So yes, apart from that, Kelowna is amazing. It's like Vancouver, only cheaper, and the weather is better and that's always a major pull.

We stay at a B&B on Ethel Street with a lovely Dutch couple called Ed and Brigitte Monster, although they use Brigitte's maiden name instead as they have a baby called Damien...wise move I would say. Not so wise with the first name choice perhaps at the time, but blame baby brain and all that.

They moved to Kelowna in Spring 2007 and love it. They came for a more relaxed lifestyle and to spend more time together, and they say they've got that with the B&B and her graphic design company. It seems they are making things work. Makes me think again that Nathan and I really should start our own business.

We eat out at Earls, go for a stroll along the beaches, drive along the coast and then the next day, after more exploring and buying the local paper to check out where to buy and not to buy, and my favourite past time of seeing where the murders and robberies happen so we don't buy in those areas, we decide it's time to head back.

Kelowna has lived up to our expectations. I can imagine buying a house here, with a yard and two dogs...hey, wasn't that the plan all along?

(Meanwhile . . . a few days later, still in May . . .)

So I'm on the computer, my nbf since coming out to Canada, and I get an email from Big White Ski Resort. No silly, not the mountain, but its peeps. The vice president says he would like to make contact about any marketing ideas I would have to get their name out there, particularly in England and Germany.

You see I contacted Big White a few months back saying that although I know there are no jobs at the moment, I would love to move to the Okanagan and that my love of snowboarding, plus my passion for writing would mean I could help them market themselves.

In true Canadian style, they DID keep my profile, and get in contact when they had something!

So it gets me thinking. I've been to Clearwater and they need promotion, Big White wants promotion, and Grouse Mountain was talking about promoting themselves in the run up to the Olympics in 2010.

It seems that all the resorts want to ride the wave of the Olympics, but aren't sure how.

Nathan and I have often discussed in one of our many "we should have our own business" discussions about starting a magazine in Canada for resorts to market themselves. After going for the Clearwater job, I realize that we could well market these kinds of resorts because we have a passion for it and the media and sales skills. EUREKA! We could be a resort marketing team, couldn't we?

As I venture upstairs to tell Nathan my cunning plan, he has just walked out of the bathroom, half shaven and says the exact same thing.

This is the land of opportunity.

That book, *Secrets of the Millionaire Mind*, says to take a risk and think big. Why the hell not? We've got a name, Go! Lifestyle Marketing. Now, if we can just get Big White as our first client, we are laughing.

Nathan could give up work, my job could bring in the money for now and we could really get this off the ground. With his sales skills, my media contacts and writing, and our passion for the outdoors, this, my Dear Watson, could be just the key. I just have a feeling I should be running my own business with Nathan by my side.

That would eventually mean we could live anywhere and yes, have a house, a yard and a couple of dogs to boot. Did I say that already? Again, that's the ultimate goal, right? And since being in Canada, I realize we need to make the money before we can achieve that goal. It's not quite as simple as we had imagined. Go figure.

***

Chapter 32

PHONING HOME

I've just been on the phone to my mum and dad in Spain for 90 minutes and then my sister, another 90 minutes. It's the only time I can talk for hours on the phone, otherwise I think the phone has one use, to make arrangements of when and where to meet. Oh, and interviewing people for stories.

When you move to another country, you can expect to dedicate a lot of phone time.

It seems the recession is starting to be felt in Europe. Food prices have gone up, especially on wheat products, house prices are dropping, and people are getting worried.

It's quite a tough time. I wasn't old enough to truly understand the Thatcher years, but this gives me just a taster. It's quite frightening.

Canada is saying that the Olympics, plus the fact that we (get me calling myself Canadian already) have healthy trade relations with Asia, among other things, means we will only feel a ripple. It still makes you wonder whether it could be the wrong time to buy a place? When is it the right/wrong time to buy property anyway? Anyone? Anyone?

Our friends MooMoo and Courto have come to stay for a week and we have the best week ever.

We laugh for what seems like days, well, I suppose it is.

I have to admit, I miss that ease you have with old friends. The history. They are like family. It's something that you only get with time.

By the end of the week I'm so sad to see them go, but I'm just so pleased that our friends are coming out to see us. It means so much when you are this far away. Just goes to show that distance doesn't really come between true friends in the end.

***

Chapter 33

FAMILY FEUDS

Nathan has spoken to his brother.

I think it came as a bit of a shock really. He always thought his brother was against his dad's relationship, however, it seems he has come to accept that as long as his dad is happy, well, that's the main thing.

This makes sense in so many ways, but I can also understand why Nathan is still angry. If someone had hurt my parents the way his dad had been hurt, then I would get protective too. And Nathan is of Italian descent, and you know what they say, don't mess with the family. Neighhh.

What seems to have come from this chat however, is that Nathan is no longer talking about flying home and giving them a piece of his mind. I'm not sure how they'd feel about a criminal record in Canada! He has actually turned into a little boy of late. I feel sorry for him. He looks lost. How come men can be so much like children one minute and the next they are running around gorilla style all alpha-like.

I decide that perhaps it is time for me to step in and try and smooth things over.

I really don't want their relationship to go sour; family is so important. So I email his dad, telling him how much Nathan loves him and that it's because he cares that he got so mad. Basically it's an email to say we are thinking of him.

I ask Nathan if it's OK to send it; he says, yea whatever.

It works.

The next day, Nathan pops out for a run, and the phone rings. It's his dad. It's 2am in the UK. His dad says he was just off to the bathroom, and thought he would try us. Bless him. We end up having a chat, and I tell him Nathan is just concerned. Nathan gets home, and they chat. It's still a little awkward, but it's better, and they are talking again. Nathan tells him he won't be returning for the wedding.

Sometimes, there are great benefits of living thousands of miles away as I think the dad believes that's the reason.

***

Chapter 34

FIRST DAY, NEW JOB NERVES
(May 2008)

It's the first day of my new job at Bunkerworld.

I feel like I am actually getting used to starting new jobs now. It is becoming less daunting, but that still doesn't mean I get any sleep the night before. I always think I'm OK, but I end up looking at the clock every 30 minutes. What is it with the body clock? How come, even when you've set countless alarms, you end up picking up your watch every half hour on the dot, without fail in that panic "oh my goodness I am going to be late" mode?

So I eventually get up at 7am. I've never been great at early mornings, even during my days on radio.

Let's just say, at the last newspaper I worked at, the joke was, don't talk to Nat before 10am! It seems in Canada this is changing, and I am seeing the benefits of early mornings.

I drag myself out of bed, have a quick shower and get to the bus stop 15 minutes early. I feel like a true city commuter. I arrive at work 30 minutes before I'm meant to and fill my time by basically walking up and down Granville Street.

I look like one of the homeless people by the end of it because it's so damn hot (in May, crazy, especially considering it was snowing a few days ago) and I've put on a ton of clothes in case the weather turns. Give me a shopping trolley and a mutt on a string and I would fit right in. *(Sidenote: Sadly, there are more than 2,200 homeless in Vancouver, and the problem, like any big city, is just getting worse.)*

I'm standing outside, trying to find the number to call the office upstairs, because we still haven't got a mobile phone yet. Crazy, right? It has been pretty liberating to be honest not having a cell phone (better get with the lingo), and I am loath to give that up right now. Plus, cell phone plans are expensive in Canada, with Canadians paying one of the highest rates in the world due to the area the network needs to cover. There is also limited competition due to regulatory barriers that make it difficult for new companies. For most people, $50 a month which includes 1GB of data is cheap as chips. So yes, a cell phone can wait.

Where was I? Oh yes, standing in the lobby, trying to figure out how to get into my new office.

Suddenly I get cornered by a guy who is a little, well, odd. He tells me he owns a publishing company. Aha, never judge by appearance Nat!

My boss arrives just as the guy is giving me his card, asking if I want a job! Great timing. I decide not to try and explain because I am really not interested in another job right now.

We go upstairs and the next eight hours go by in a bit of a blur.

Have I made a mistake or is this just first day nerves? It looks like I'm going to be writing about fuel and oil, not ships and the environment. There's so much to learn as well. It's all percentages this, and dollars per barrel that, and mixing solutions and fuel grades.

The guys in the office are amazing however. They are so patient and relaxed, but there's just the two of them, in a very small office. I can't help but wonder if I may have backed myself in a corner.

I've moved to a new country. I work in an office that consists of three people, one of them is me, and I'm writing about something I know nothing about.

Nothing quite like throwing yourself in at the deep end.

I've just written a story about a double-hull ship and rising fuel prices.

I get home and I chat to Nathan musing out loud that I hope I don't regret my decision. He looks pretty annoyed with me, so I don't push it. What on earth am I going to do? He is kind of relying on me right now to bring in the money while he looks for a job. I feel the pressure.

Next day.

Great day at work. I love my new job! Bring it on.

One week in and my job is going really well. I'm really starting to get the hang of it now, and it looks like the company wants me to really expand on the environmental topics. I've been looking into how to reduce pollution from ships, I've been talking to people in Barbados, Hawaii, Florida, Texas, Japan, Hong Kong, you name it.

The week consists of going on a "family lunch" with the team, which means a two-hour lunch on Friday on the company, writing countless stories, and getting recognition in, get this, the Wall Street Journal. Oh and did I mention we listen to music in the office? Yes, my boss loves playing music and it's such a great inspirational tool, especially when there are so few of us. It kind of fills the silence.

Both Martin and Guy are really into music too, and we've all got similar tastes, which stems from Metallica to Simon & Garfunkel. I should have known because one of the questions at my original interview was "do you like Rush and which album do you consider the best?" 2112 of course.

As a team we've even decided we may start a company band called Bad Sushi, appropriate because Vancouver is the land of great sushi restaurants and I have to say, I've yet to have bad sushi, and together, I am sure we would be terrible. You know how these things escalate, especially when you've found your tribe. Ideas just get silly and everyone gets carried away.

I've started building up partnerships with people at NOAA, the United Nations, educational facilities, scientists, you name it. I have huge plans for the environmental section of the website that we run. I could write White Papers, build partnerships to help raise awareness, create a technology section...I have so many ideas.

There seems to be so much opportunity as well, and my boss loves my ideas. Either that, or he tells me, "let's call that Plan B," which means, not quite Nat!

I've been chatting with people in our Singapore and London offices, I'm chilling listening to Hendrix, the sun is shining and I get off work at 4ish and arrive at 8ish. I love the West Coast lifestyle. Long may it reign. Yea baby.

Monday is shite. And so it continues. Up and down like a bride's nightie. I've come to realize that Monday and Tuesday are pants and the rest of the week the leads for stories come in and I get to write some super cool stories. I'm actually becoming a bit of a geek as well. It's all starting to make a lot more sense now. They talk about fuel costing an arm and a leg, well when a cruise ship is spending $13 million on fuel, it's just a drop in the ocean.

I've been cycling to work every day and I seem to be getting super fit. That's the West Coast for you.

Mind you, this morning I was cycling along, scooting in and out of the traffic, when I looked to my side and this guy is so busy looking over at something he fails to notice the car has stopped in front. He slams on his brakes and flies over the handle bars. He misses the car by millimetres. Isn't it awful when you don't know what to do. Do I stop and see if he's OK, or carry on? I know I should stop, but I still question it. Why? He's OK, just a little shaken up, poor guy.

I decide to not be a city person and ignore it, and go over to check on him. He is fine. Just a little embarrassed. I'm honestly not sure I would have done the same in the UK for fear of being shouted at. Here, it seems more natural to run over to help people and check to see if they are all good.

Nathan is going through a bit of a, how shall I call it, moment right now. If he were a girl, I'd say he has PMS. He's been down, I mean seriously down. I can only put it down to not having any joy in finding what he calls a "real" job, and then the family situation.

I can't quite snap him out of it, but I know he will get something amazing soon. Not that I say that. Patience.

My friend has invited me on an all expenses paid trip to Whistler for the weekend. What a laugh. I think being apart from Nathan could do us good. Give us something else to talk about.

(Sidenote: When it comes to cell phone plans in Canada, shop around. There are indeed limited choices, but they are getting more competitive. Expect to spend $60+ a month on a plan that includes local calls and texts and around 2GB data. Also, remember that because Canada is huge, coverage isn't always reliable, depending on where you are. If you go out of province, you may be charged, and when you cross the border to the US, your phone may not work. Read the fine print. When it comes to home data plans, while Rogers and Telus are the main suppliers, independents do offer data plans. As a guide, I pay around $160 a month for basic TV, home phone and high speed data.)

***

Chapter 35

THE HALF WAY MARK – SETTLING IN
(Still May 2008)

I call it halfway, well, we've been in Canada for, well let's see, seven months, and, well, it feels a lot longer. That's usually a bad thing because it means time is dragging, but it's definitely not. The first couple of years I think are the hardest in many ways, as you are learning so many new things (hence halfway mark). My weeks are flying by here. I've noticed a few changes in me too already during this period.

I now roll my r's ever so slightly and soften my t's (because, many Canadians don't understand me otherwise). Some Canadians call us pompous Brits and I think it is because we pronounce our Ts and it can sound that way to them.

I now no longer ask for a Mocha, as I fail to get understood, so now I have to say mow-kur, and I must admit I feel like a right idiot saying it. On the subject of food, I have to ask for yo-gurrt, instead of yoghurt, again because I may as well be speaking Swahili when I order that. I've stopped converting dollars to UK pounds – unless I'm buying something I consider expensive, and then putting it into British pounds always makes it sound cheaper.

I'm also beginning to realize that being away from family and friends does have its benefits. Don't get me wrong, I love them, but I realize now I kind of had a role as the listener and an empath.

People talk, I listen. And then I go away and worry myself silly about them, while they are fine. It got to the point where virtually everyone I met would offload. Which is great for them, but had me tearing my hair out with concern. I couldn't go out for a nice meal and talk about, say, the weather. No, no, no. It would start off with a minor rant about what the husband/boyfriend/wife had done/said and resulted in one big pissed off venting session. Dare I suggest to just not worry about it. Yikes, run and hide, run and hide.

Admittedly, sometimes it was deserved, but I discovered that it had become such a bad habit for everyone involved. Maybe I encourage it? Or maybe it was one of those cases I had read about where your friend associates you with moaning and therefore that's all they do? I realized that one day when I was sat having coffee with one friend and she said "oh, he's really pissed me off now. What did he do the other day? Umm, I know it was something. I'm sure he said something?" It clicked right there that nothing was actually wrong, aside from how we had evolved our relationship into this.

Then there was the time we went for a run and another friend vented for the entire hour. Let me tell you, before that run I felt so relaxed. An hour later and I was so stressed out.

Yes, being away does have some merits.

Nathan has even said how less stressed I seem. He said he used to dread seeing me after I'd seen some of my friends because I'd be so tightly wound up with what they'd told me. I'm a fixer, I feel I need to fix people's problems, but over the years you realize you can't and it makes you feel rather helpless. I also realize that I was at fault, as I wanted to feel needed, and so helping others and listening was a way of doing that. Not healthy. Not healthy at all.

Yes, being away definitely has its merits. You get a more holistic view of yourself.

New friends don't carry that baggage, so they won't offload because they already do that with tried and trusted old friends. That leaves me to enjoy all the goodies, like having fun.

Take last night for example. We went round my friend Zuzia's house for dinner. Her brother came over and we sat in the apartment, 16 floors up, looking out across to the City, chatting away about old stories of Nathan getting in all sorts of scraps, like the time him and his best friend were chased by a guy with road rage on their way to Heathrow airport. Nathan had no idea why the guy was so pissed off, but it ended up with the guy blocking off Nathan so he couldn't go anywhere, getting out his car, pummeling him and then his friend and driving off.

Nathan spent the entire holiday with a wonky jaw and his friend with a black eye. Sounds gruesome, but the way Nathan tells it, it's hilarious. The best bit is that only last year, Nathan's mate told him the reason the guy got road rage was because he had flicked him the bird! That story never gets old.

As we sat there, an eagle swooped over our heads. This place is pretty damn amazing and so are the people it seems.

(July 2008)

I've been in my job for a couple of months now, whoopee.

It has had its ups and downs, as any job does, but mainly its ups.

I get to phone Jamaica in the morning and speak to a woman called Cecelia who I've grown so fond of and who gave me the best quote when I asked her what people were saying about the current trend in increasing oil costs: "People are saying why, why, why, why, why, why, why?" No joke, I counted seven whys, it was great!

Sometimes her accent gets so strong and I don't quite understand her over the phone, and all I can do is picture her sat there in an office surrounded by people smoking reefers, while she shouts at people to get their arses in gear.

I know also that sometimes when I say something, she has no clue what I said as my accent must be so strong to her too. But she laughs, I laugh, we carry on.

I've also made friends with a guy in New Orleans called Terry who sounds like a real oil baron and has that fantastic drawl. I can't say our conversations are always about oil, in fact last week he told me about a neighbour who had won the lottery. How she travelled from Brazil after her husband had died, and had a tough time, but how now she's living the life of Riley. Well he didn't quite say that, as that's so English, but it involved the words "awesome," "stoked," "man," and "yee-haw" (I made that last one up).

(August 2008)

Nathan and I have reached a goal. The rules in
Canada are that after three months of payslips you
can get a mortgage. So we were waiting for one of
us to get in a good paying job, before we started
looking for a place to live.

Nathan has started a new job working on products
for the Olympics, so it won't take long for him to
catch up now. We book an appointment to see our
friendly account manager at the bank.

I lock my bike up outside the bank, roll my trouser
leg down and meet Nathan at the front. How
exiting! Our very first place could soon become a
reality.

Our account manager comes to get us, about 40
minutes after our appointment time – you can tell
we've fitted into the lifestyle already. We hardly bat
an eyelid at the delay, it's just the Vancouver way.

We explain to her that we are interested in looking
into getting a mortgage.

Apparently, with permanent residents, you need to
be able to put down quite a large deposit, which we
already knew and why we didn't dare dip into our
savings. You also need to make sure you're out of
your probationary period at work. We tell her that's
fine as I'm approaching my three months. She
warns us that some companies have a year

probationary period in Canada! We ask her if the 2.5 times your wages idea applies in Canada, and she tells us that it all depends.

Basically, mortgage lenders work it out on a variety of things like your outgoings such as leases and credit card bills every month, the condo fees if applicable for the new property and any other amounts that would impact your final disposable income. Then they take into account what you'd need to live off for food etc. and then it all gets worked out from there. That means, if you're good with your money, you can get more dollars. If, however, your account shows you're a spendthrift, then you'll have a little more trouble. It's basically down to your credit rating and we were wise enough to get a credit card as soon as we landed.

Also, we find out that you can do a little bit of haggling. If you find a better rate elsewhere, some banks will match it.

We leave feeling happy that we know what we're up against.

I say we, what I mean is Nathan. If I'm honest, I haven't got a clue what I'm talking about when it comes to mortgages. Nathan owned a place outside of London once, so he's done this before. Me, I feel like an air head, and by the end of the conversation, I can see she's looking at me like a school teacher with boatload of patience. I do leave feeling a little bit wiser however. Just a wee bit.

I just want someone to say, this is how much you can have, this is how much I need back from you each month and et voila, a nice house with a picket fence, a front porch and suddenly a rocking chair appears in front of me with my name on it. I suppose I'm the investor at this point!

I go home and do my research on buying your first home in BC.

In short. This is the best advice for buying your first home in BC:

First decide, do you want to go with a mortgage lender or broker?
Basically a bank versus an individual. Just be sure they are trusted.

Now it's time for the pre-approval process (before you start looking at all the homes you can't afford).
For this, you need proof of employment and earnings (keep those wage slips), a credit rating check, an understanding of how much downpayment you need (something to keep an eye on because even if you have 20% the increasing interest rates mean you will be put under a stress test to see if you can handle it financially). If you don't have 20% downpayment, you will more than likely need to pay insurance to cover your butt...which can add up.

Now pick the brains of your mortgage lender.
Ask all the questions, even if you think they are stupid. Ask how strata fees impact your mortgage, what insurances you need to consider, their

predictions for interest rates, the benefits of bimonthly versus monthly payments,. And ask, ask, ask, about variable and fixed mortgages, term lengths, and above all, what fees are included if you want to pay it off early or, at the end of the term, decide not to go back with them. Those hidden fees can be crazy!

Ask friends.
Get advice from friends who already have mortgages!

(Sidenote: As of June 2019, if your down payment is 20% or more of the property value, you'll get a conventional mortgage. If your down payment is less than 20%, you'll get a high-ratio mortgage, which requires mortgage default insurance.)

***

Chapter 36

STILL PROPERTY SEARCHING
(March 2009)

Fast forward to property buying time. Exciting!

Location, location, location. However if you want to live in Vancouver that, like other major cities means money, money, money.

There's a few problems you face when looking into properties in Vancouver. The most notorious one is the leaky condo. Most places in Canada are wood frame buildings and many of those buildings have been constructed in the winter, when it is wet and raining, you get the idea. This has led to a glut of properties with leaking roofs, gutters, sidings, you name it.

You've really got to do your digging to make sure you don't get stuck with a property that needs a new roof, and that's highly likely if you happen to fall in love with one of the New England-style homes here. There's a saying here that homes built in the 1950s are strong, those built in the 70s and 80s have plenty of issues, and the new homes, well, despite being constructed to meet building code, the pitfall is you will have to pay GST on the price tag (that's the general sales tax).

There's always the Vancouver Specials, which are very bog standard looking homes, but we just aren't keen on those.

Another problem is noise pollution.

We start our property search. Our dream of owning a home in BC is within touching distance now.

But where do we move to? Well, North Vancouver is cool. We liked it there and it's close to the mountains. I kind of like Kerrisdale as it has a cute town centre. Marpole is a nice area, great little spots there. South Granville, that's nice too. Kitsilano, that's probably out of our price range. Up by the University of British Columbia, yes, I like that. Cool. But some places are on Native land, so you have to be aware of additional leasing etc.

Plenty of options.

Too many it seems. We just happen to come across a realtor while attending an open house (they hold lots here at the weekends, and you basically look for the sign "Open House" sign and wander on in), and, well as far as we understand it, you need to get a realtor. We tell him the areas we are looking at and you see he is thinking, oh jeez, what do I have here? They can't narrow it down a little?

It turns out there are hundreds upon hundreds of places in our price range in those areas, and actually going back and forth across the bridge all the time for work would be a nightmare. So we decide to focus on the downtown Vancouver neighbourhoods.

We attend open house after open house. You can find these on property websites like remax and rew. The search is never ending, and oh my gawd there are some shitholes out there. Either they have had the worst refurbishments in the world ever, or they are part of the leaky condo crisis. This, as I mentioned, is basically considered the construction, legal and financial hell of Canada in which buildings built between 1980 and 2000 had that severe damage by rainwater infiltration. Not something you want to be a part of. Big fees. Huge.

Just when we start to get property search fatigue, our realtor takes us to a townhouse in South Granville. We don't know that much about the area, but it looks nice.

The townhouse is one of four. Basically it was an old house, or mansion really, converted into four two-bedroom plus den townhomes. The marketing online for the place is just awful...it's a photo of the front door. We have no idea what to expect.

We walk in and I am struck by the place. Oh, don't get me wrong, it's in terrible condition but there is so much potential. I am already redesigning in my mind. You could knock down this wall, open up this area, replace those bits, update the kitchen, create another bathroom. My mind is in overdrive. As we walk up three flights of steps to a patio that looks over some tennis courts and the North Shore mountains, I am sold. This is it.

Nathan, however, is seeing an old, neglected home that has small rooms, a weird layout and is just, well, pretty disgusting.

As we walk out and get into the car I turn to him and start describing what we could do with this place. I see a spark in his eyes, and as we are about to drive off, he says, "I don't think I gave that house the credit it deserves. Can we go back?" And so we get out of the car, go back in and I start telling him what I see. You can see the wheels start to turn. His eyes are suddenly open. By Jove, I think he's got it!

We go back to our apartment after that and sit there, trying to work out how much we would want to offer. We decide to put in a cheeky offer the next day, because, well, its the Brit way I suppose, and get turned down.

We are a little concerned about going in too high. It's our first property purchase, and you never quite know what you are doing. What if we can't afford the monthly payments? What if we have unexpected bills? Will we go bankrupt? Eventually we speak to Nathan's dad. Always great for business advice. He asks us if we can afford to make the monthly payments. With my wage we definitely can at a stretch, and with Nathan's on top, that would give us the extra we needed. He says, "well what are you thinking about then?"

The next day we make our offer and it gets accepted. We receive final approval from the bank for the mortgage. My parents offer to give us some money to get us to a point where we won't pay the additional insurance for not having quite enough downpayment. We find a lawyer to do the paperwork, who actually works in the same building as me. Convenient. We get a property inspection to ensure we know what we are letting ourselves in for (advised at all costs and in this case it was around $1,000), and I go over the paperwork with a fine tooth comb, and pick the lawyer up on a few things she has missed.

We have bought our first place. A townhouse at that, for $445,000.

(Sidenote: If you are reading this in 2019, that price will make you gulp as the average price for a townhouse around that area is $1 million. Crazy.)

(June 2011)

Fast forward two years.

OK, so why am I skipping two whole years of my life again? Two whole years? What went on? Well, life I suppose.

It's funny how what was once new becomes the norm. You eat, sleep, work, play, repeat. Everything becomes more familiar and everything in the UK sounds more alien. And yet I look back and really so much has happened.

Nathan was working for a sports company that was dealing with Olympic merchandise and we met the most amazing people through his work. The 2010 Winter Olympics was an amazing time to be in Vancouver and made even more amazing by his connections. We were fortunate enough to see a lot of the events, including the half pipe where Shaun White pulled off the first ever Double McTwist 1260 (Tomahawk) to win Gold. We watched the hockey, the bobsleigh, you name it. That was in between hanging around on Granville Street while soaking up the atmosphere and helping him restock at the stores (because they were running out of merchandise so quickly).

Vancouver was alive. Truly alive. And I think those who opted to head out of the city during that time truly missed out on a fantastic experience. I highly recommend sticking around if your city wins the bid for the Olympics.

After that, Nathan got a job for the Vancouver Canucks, our local hockey team, as the retail manager. Pretty cool. We got to see countless hockey games and concerts while he was there, but bless him, he was pulling long hours. It was so wonderful to see him grow however.

Me, I quickly went from an analyst at Bunkerworld, to the editor and brand manager on their sustainability brand where I got to work closely with scientists, government officials and the shipping industry on creating new legislations and white papers.

I was suddenly flying off to Washington, London (and catching up with friends and family) and Miami. It was a fantastic job, and so very fulfilling. I grew so much during my time there, because they allowed me to bring ideas to the table and implement them with a highly skilled team.

I ended up looking after an entire editorial team, creating new technology websites, and eventually I was promoted to director of the company within the space of less than two years. Canada really does promote growth in the workplace, that's for sure.

I somehow went from having a few tools in my toolbox to so, so many, thanks to those I worked with and who mentored me.

In between work, because, well life is about more than work right (but at least we were established now), we were having our annual vacation to Hawaii (it's so bizarre saying that as, coming from the UK, Hawaii is just so far away and somewhere you doubt you will ever get to. But here in Canada, it's like Brits going to Spain).

I say it was our annual vacation because at 10 days holiday a year here in Canada (which is what many companies will start you on), we could only take one holiday really.

(Sidenote: On the vacation leave thing, generally, you will earn vacation leave for each month you receive 75 hours or 10 days' pay, but this can vary according to your collective agreement or classification group. As a new employee you are entitled to vacation leave with pay in the amount of your earned vacation credits, but if you have completed six months of continuous employment, you are entitled to receive an advance of credits equivalent to the anticipated credits you will earn in the current fiscal year. A fiscal year is defined as April 1 to March 31. Thanks Government of Canada for that info. In addition, each province has stat holidays, which us Brits calls bank holidays. Employees who work on a statutory holiday are entitled to extra pay or time off in lieu.)

We had managed to renovate our house in South Granville. We had builders come in to open the place up and put a beam through the centre to give it an open plan feel. We replaced the kitchen and installed a washroom, and then the painting, replacement of doors, baseboards, and all those minor things we did all ourselves. We even learned how to mud walls and lay floors!

By the time we had finished, it was a different house. It was gorgeous . . . and we wanted to move, because, well, I suppose that is us, and yes, of course we did. Always onto the next thing it seems.

We had contracted the renovation bug (careful, that's a thing), and while every evening and weekend was spent refurbishing the place (Home Depot was our second home, which is kind of like Homebase), and we were tired when it was done, for some reason we just wanted to do it all again. It was so satisfying, and we continued learning, every single day..

Quite honestly, the mountains and North Vancouver were calling. The reason we came to Canada never left us. We just wanted to be out of the city, which was quickly growing, and to be even closer to nature. Plus, we could make a healthy $150k on the place we were in, which would allow us to buy a house. Our own detached place!

And so, we put the townhouse on the market. Had a few interested buyers who messed us around quite a bit, so much so that we actually took it off the market for a few weeks and decided maybe we shouldn't sell. But then we got a serious offer.

It was time to start house hunting again. We tried to renew our mortgage with the bank, or just switch it, but they wanted to charge us astronomical fees whether we stayed with them or went elsewhere. So we went elsewhere!

(*Note previous advice about finding out about these fees before getting a mortgage.)

We also chose to go with the realtors who listed our home to search for property (thanks Faith Wilson). They had a dedicated person who just helped with with property searching, and Maggie, the lady who helped us, was amazing. Such a laugh and she had the vision too. She just got us.

We spent the next few weeks looking at homes all across North Vancouver. Again, either I was highly suspect that the houses have been used as a Marijuana grow-op – which not only can be a problem because they cause moisture in the house, but can increase your insurance premiums, that is, if you can get a mortgage on it – or they were just crapshoots. Like serious dives.

It was getting painful, as property hunting can be. And when one of us did eventually like a place, the other wasn't so keen. That wasn't like us. But we always agreed we both had to like it.

Ideally we wanted a house with a rental suite downstairs that would help offset the mortgage. Something over near Lonsdale with a couple of bathrooms at least. And then one day we walked into this little two-bed, one bath rancher in Lynn Valley, and just, well, fell in love.

It was owned by a beautiful older lady who had lost her husband, and it really was a classic 1950s home. Small rooms, a little run down for sure, but there was so much love felt in the house, and, we could rip down all the walls and open it up. We moved to Canada for space, and space is what we wanted.

We were sold. I can't quite explain it. I was sold a little more than Nathan, but only fractionally. We went back three times, and yes, it was dark, but as I explained to Nathan, if you opened up the walls it would be a completely different story.

So we made an offer. Again, a little cheeky, but when the inspection report came back it needed everything doing to it, and I mean everything! The inspector told us he had never seen an electrical panel and system like this. The retaining wall was falling down. The roof was old. There was possible asbestos. The list went on and on. And yet, it didn't phase us in the least. There was just something about this place.

Sold for $645,000 to the pompous Brits.

TIPS ON SELLING A HOUSE IN BC
Check out comparable properties in the area
Do your research to see what properties are being listed at that are similar to yours, or what they have sold for, so you have realistic expectations. Just because you spent $150,000 on renovations doesn't mean it will add that to your property value. It may be more, hopefully, if you have been wise.

Documents
Gather all the necessary documents: deeds, surveys, property tax receipts, renovation contracts, warranties, etc.

Decide if you want a realtor to do it or list it privately
Listing it privately isn't something I would recommend, unless you have plenty of time on your hands and have a great property lawyer, but, it can save you so much money. It is tempting to go with a

one percent realtor to avoid the fees, and honestly, I have had friends work as agents for these company and it can be great. But my honest advice is, see which realtor is hot in your area. Which one seems to be moving properties quickly and whose face is on every billboard on every front lawn. There's a reason for that. Now you have a rough idea of the price you want and should expect, get a few realtors in to give you their estimates.

Additional Fees
Remember, you won't get the price that is on the tin! The realtor gets their percentage, the lawyer will get theirs, there will be a statement of adjustment and possibly a mortgage discharge fee/prepayment fee as well. Just be aware of all the additional fees so you can be mindful, however, the lawyer/solicitor will sort that for you. The lawyer will also figure out how much property tax you have paid and how much you will get reimbursed.

Patience
We have got so used to a market where houses are sold within a day of being listed, that now, when it takes two weeks, or sometimes more, we instantly think about dropping the price. If you can wait, don't do that. If you have been reasonable, someone will come along and you might even see a bidding war on your hands.

Is This Your Principal Residence?
If not, and you have been renting this one out and living in another, please, please, please, read up on Capital Gains. It can be massive, so pay an accountant to tell you your options.

***

Chapter 37

BACK TO OUR ROOTS
(The year 2013)

The next few years went by in a blur, again. Funny
how that happens. We were just always on the go,
snowboarding throughout the winter, and
continuing to instruct on the mountain in the
evenings for a free pass, mountain biking in the
summer and exploring, working hard, chilling with
great mates, family visits, and then there was the
house renovation.

We were experiencing one of the coldest winters
that Vancouver had been through in years and we
were living in a place that had been stripped to its
bare bones. It had nothing but four walls and a
partial roof, and we loved it. We would sit in bed at
night with four sweaters on each, toques (that's hats
or beanies to us Brits), and three duvets, and laugh
as we saw our breath in the air above. It was so
much fun and what an experience. The construction
crew was making bets on when we would
eventually cave in and go to a hotel.

We didn't. Not even when we didn't have a toilet for
a few days! Don't ask. You see, this was our baby.

Remember that chap that owned the car dealership I
told you about at the beginning of the book? Well,
he offered Nathan a position in sales and Nathan

had decided being a retail sales manager wasn't for him. He missed cars far too much.

My time working as a director for someone else's business was coming to an end. All I wanted to do was write and not get caught up in office politics and paperwork, and I was offered a job for a publishing firm as an editor looking after seven different magazines.

I had done my time as a director, and I no longer wanted to be a director of someone else's business. My love was writing and editing. I had proven to myself I could do it, to rise through the ranks, to organise events, market companies, write white papers, work on legislative documents, build websites, sort out accounts and HR, and now I wanted to go back to what I love. I had nothing to prove. From my experience in the shipping sector, I had this bright idea to start up a fun side business doing content marketing for people in the shipping industry with my colleague Guy, and we were starting to work on that "hobby" as we called it.

My full time day job was now with a family run business, and despite being thrown in at the deep end due to some unfortunate circumstances, it was an amazing company filled with incredibly talented people. And they even gave me stat holidays off. We finished work early on Fridays, and it just reminded me of the newspaper where I used to work.

It was another steep learning curve, but such an amazing company where I was learning about credit unions, universities in Canada, First Nation history, renewable energy, you name it. I was truly learning about Canada. Delving deep into this land I loved.

Life was pretty sweet really.

(2013/2014)

And then along came Calgary.

What can I say about this? Honestly, I find it incredibly hard to know where to start.

Things were going so well, I mean, we had a great work/life balance, we were happy, so very happy. We were always looking to new challenges, to renovate more, and while we didn't yet have our remote house in the boonies (the name we give places here for being in the middle of nowhere), we were on our way and enjoying every minute.

So Calgary . . . let's go back a few years to give you context.

Calgary was never really on our radar. The rockies were stunning, but Calgary itself was not really a consideration. In 2012 however, Nathan's boss had mentioned to him that he was thinking of opening a dealership in Cowtown (that's Calgary) and there could be a position coming up.

When he told me we both laughed. We lived five minutes from the mountains in BC. Why would we move to Calgary? A place that BC referred to as a city full of "steers and queers." Thanks An Officer and a Gentleman for that one (and sorry Calgarians, we jest). But really, it wasn't a city we were interested in due to its proximity to the mountains and the more money-driven lifestyle.

So when Nathan came home a couple of years later and said that his boss had offered him the role as general sales manager at the new Calgary dealership, what did I think? Well, I laughed. Of course I laughed.

He didn't.

Wait, what? We had built an amazing community of friends here now. We didn't need to chase money in a city that didn't have what we had come to Canada for. We loved renovating, and we wanted to do it all again. I loved my job. My own side business was really really taking off. I was getting more clients every day. He worked with amazing people. We were snowboarding after work, swimming in the canyon down the road, hiking in the rainforest, doing everything we had dreamt of...but wait...honestly, what was that serious expression on his face?

For the next three weeks Nathan refused to talk to me. I tried, but nothing. I tried the cold shoulder too, for a day (ooh go me), but that of course didn't work. Was he really playing the silent treatment game? And sleeping in a different bed to prove a point? What on earth was going on?

The only reason he came back into our bedroom was that we had some friends coming to stay. And then he put in the effort.

When they were gone, finally, I cracked. I hate not talking and this was getting ridiculous. I asked him again what he thought and he told me he would resent me for not giving it even a second thought. Resent? That's rather harsh, no? I mean, OK. Maybe I should give this more consideration if it meant that much to him and not have laughed at the idea, but we had laughed years earlier about the exact same scenario? I suppose things change, if anything, Canada has taught me a lot about that.

So I thought about it. And I thought about it. And I thought about it.

I had left the UK, all my friends and family and moved to a new land, where I had new friends who were now becoming old friends and family. I was loving our life. I would have to do this all again, leave my own business and a city I absolutely adore as well? But, I was torn because I should at least be open to it.

And so I told Nathan, that in order to make a decision, I would need to go back out to Calgary (I had been once many years ago). He told me it would be a waste of money and that I already had it in my head that it was a firm no. To be fair, it wasn't. I can be extremely stubborn, I admit that, but if this meant that much to him I needed to better understand what would be ahead of me.

So eventually, with a lot of persuasion, he booked flights to Calgary during January. He organized with some friends out there to show us around. We arrived and it was minus 35! OK, I can handle the cold...can't I? Now, where did my nose go?

One of Nathan's friends knew about my love of nature, and took me to places you could go mountain biking or hiking, but it was hard to get a feel for it when it was covered in snow and ice, and aside from the distant rockies, it looked so very flat (and I'm not a flat earther). The mountains...they just seemed so very, very far away compared to what we were used to.

I tried to stop comparing Calgary to Vancouver. I had to. Could I do this? For just a couple of years maybe? Yes. Yes I could do anything for him. I could. But could I?

When we came back from the trip, I told him that if he agreed to two years maximum, then I would be up for it. Deal done! Sold to the lady without a nose.

This was a couple of years before the dealership would open. And things dramatically changed during that time. The start of the change came after a conversation with a guy I knew, Nathan let slip that he had agreed with his boss to four years in Calgary and not two.

He had failed to inform me it seems. I admit, I was shocked. Why wouldn't he talk to me about that? I also felt silly as I didn't know any of this and found out because he let it slip to someone we knew. He dismissed my concerns.

I started to feel very low. Low about the idea of leaving everything I had dreamed of and all the wonderful people that I had met behind, having to start over again in a town whose economy is focussed on oil, and leave my own business and business partner behind. No more evening snowboarding sessions on Grouse Mountain, mountain biking on Fromme just two minutes from my door, no more swims in the canyons with bears roaming wildly around me. Yes, it wasn't quite the "simple life" I had originally intended, but it was pretty darn close, and we were still being able to afford to fly back to the UK, or spoil ourselves occasionally.

And then, one day, as I stood at the bottom of Whistler mountain looking up at my friends snowboarding down, I cried. I cried hard. I didn't want to go. I really didn't want to leave my home. But I really didn't want to disappoint my husband.

I needed to talk to Nathan. A real indepth, heart on sleeve talk. But picking the right time with him was tricky. And so, of course the opportunity came at the airport while on our way to Hawaii. Yes Nat...great thinking. Good lordy, you really do know how to pick your timing.

As we sat having a Caeser (a drink with vodka and clam juice, a caesar mix, hot sauce, and Worcestershire sauce, and served with ice in a large, celery salt-rimmed glass...a bit like a Bloody Mary for the Brits), I explained my concerns.

He was so angry. To be expected in many ways really as he had his heart set on it. So I decided to ask him the one question that meant everything to me and would in fact answer my biggest fear. "If I get super down after six months or so, could we come back to BC?"

His answer shocked me. "No, I wouldn't want to upset my boss."

WTF? Seriously. WTF? I had left Spain, where I really enjoyed my job and where my parents were, because Nathan was super low. Because if it wasn't working for him, it wasn't working for us. That's a marriage, right? I hadn't given that a second thought. And so, I suppose, his response, whether it was reactionary or not, gave me a glimpse of something that perhaps I had been blind to.

I cried. Damn you tears. I was in shock. What was I meant to do with that statement? His boss was his number one? Nathan didn't want to talk about it. He said, "let's ignore this and enjoy the holiday. We can talk when we are back."

I decided, OK, I will enjoy this holiday, as it could well be my last one with Nathan, who knows? I mean that was the reality here wasn't it? Who knows. And enjoy it I did. Long runs alone on the beach, swimming in shark infested waters. I really didn't care. I didn't realize then, but the black dog was following me around. But Hawaii has an amazing talent for reaching into your soul and soothing every single fibre of your being. And providing clarity.

We returned from the holiday and Nathan actually avoided me for two weeks. He would find every excuse to be out of the house and not talk. Eventually I caught him off guard when he came home I said, "let's go for a drive."

And then we chatted. On the beach in West Vancouver, looking at the ocean and watching the kayakers row by, with our ice creams in our hands. I told him I couldn't go to Calgary knowing now that my feelings weren't even a consideration. His head almost exploded as he asked if I was making him choose between his job and our marriage.

I was shocked.

I told him no, that there were other options, like a long distance relationship. I felt we were strong enough and if his desire was that strong to go, we could work this out. We could work anything out. As he drove home at a ridiculous speed, I told him to drive as fast as he wanted. It didn't scare me. I knew then and there he had chosen his job. And now it was whether he was willing to try and make things work long distance.

***

Chapter 38

THE BIG BLACK DOG
(September 2014)

As I stood on the bridge in Lynn Valley and looked over the edge, I felt in my heart it would be better if you know, I just wasn't here anymore.

I had fallen into a dark space and I had stayed there for so long that I no longer knew a way out. How dare I feel this way? How dare I? What kind of person was I? I have a wonderful family, amazing friends, I am successful, I was living a privileged life. Who was I to think this way. So selfish. Disgusting. I was disgusted at myself. Disgusted.

Looking back now, it's easy to see how gradually I sunk into that depression. So gradual in fact that when it was almost too late, I was almost in too deep.

You hear that depression hits people who have experienced a tragic childhood or experienced trauma, or used substances. What you don't hear is that anyone, absolutely anyone can fall victim to depression.

I was hanging around with a friend (I use that term loosely) who wasn't good for my soul and he made me question my entire self. It started with the odd accusing text, that I put down to my friend having an "off day" and it gradually grew worse. And yet I was clinging on because this was the only person I could talk to, or so I thought. He wasn't to blame, but he wasn't helping. I was shutting out my real friends who actually did care, because I felt I didn't deserve them.

I had shut myself down.

On the outside, friends, real friends, thought I was just distracted by the big move and the things that had been going on. Afterall, I was still able to get myself out of bed in the morning. I was functioning well at work. I was exercising, lots. I was smiling. On the outside.

Have you ever heard of smiling depression? No? Neither had I.

No-one knew. I kept it all locked deep, so deep inside. I felt like my world was crumbling. I wasn't important to the man who meant the most to me in my entire life, my dream, our dream, well the goal posts had dramatically changed, and I had a small throat cancer scare, but that turned out ok, and some good friends had passed away unexpectedly, and, and. But how dare I feel this way? And no-one deserved to see me this way.

It was a slippery slope. I tried to talk to Nathan just one time about it, and he dismissed it. Perhaps because he had been exactly there years earlier and was frightened of going back there. Perhaps my approach was too flippant. It was embarrassing.

That time was a blur. I was a zombie inside.

Nothing mattered anymore. And while I would try to berate myself for feeling this way and being so ridiculous, that just made it worse.

I just couldn't get rid of this chain around my neck. It was very dark in here. No self help book, yoga, no ridiculous amount of exercise was helping. I should have realized then it wasn't a phase. But if you've ever been there, you will know that you just aren't, well *you* when you are depressed. You're someone you don't like. In fact, you're someone you hate.

And so I gathered all the house documents together and filed them neatly so Nathan could easily access them. I tidied the house, and I went for that run. The run that took me to the bridge.

I wanted to be free of this, this thing. I wanted it to go away. Please god make it go away. I didn't want to feel this way any more.

I stood there, on that bridge, alone, and went to take the step.

Flash.

As clear as you are reading this, I saw an image of my parents and my sister. I saw a slit in that dark cloud. And my mind felt some clarity. Imagine what my parents, my beautiful loving parents, and my angel sister's lives would be like if I did this? It would destroy them.

And that. That right there made me stop. They saved me.

I could never, ever hurt them. They were my rocks. They were everything to me. I needed to stop thinking of living my life for just me, and living it for those who cared, like really cared. And this, this image is what I carry with me every single day of my life.

My parents and my sister saved my life.

The next day I called a self help line. She told me to rid myself of the friend who was making me question myself, and start with that as the first step.

That step was very crucial.

I only opened up about my depression once I had started to pull through the other side. The knock on effects when you tell people is crazy, even when you've made it out by yourself. They somehow feel that they let you down. But I hid it so well. How could they ever know? No one let me down. But I was going to get me back again, and not let myself down again either.

(Sidenote: Please, if you ever feel this way, reach out. Don't be too proud. Talk. The Crisis Intervention and Suicide Prevention Centre of British Columbia is amazing, and there are plenty of other groups, or reach out to me.)

***

Chapter 39

Nathan'S BIG MOVE
(April 2015)

I handed my notice in to work so I could focus on my business, and free up time to go and visit Nathan in Calgary.

We rented our house out in Lynn Valley for two years and I decided to move up to Squamish (in between Vancouver and Whistler), to a friend's basement suite, as it made Nathan feel more secure me being around friends. We were covering our mortgage by renting out the house, and, well, I was heading closer to the mountains.

Where did the time go?

It has been over a year since I told Nathan I wouldn't be moving to Calgary, and we decided to make this work. We promised each other, if our relationship started to fail, we would reassess. Nothing would get in the way of us. What a weird and wonderful world.

I set myself up in the basement suite and then in mid April Nathan packed his truck and left for his new life in Calgary. We were both in tears. What the hell were we doing?

Squamish was definitely an adjustment. Not only was I now working from home, in a friend's basement suite, with my blonde fluffy doggy who we had rescued a few years earlier (Nathan's idea, but he couldn't quite handle the responsibility and said she would be better off with me as I was working from home. Of course I agreed. She was my sweet doggy now and I would never abandon her). But it was so quiet compared to North Vancouver, and I didn't have my man. There were a few times I would sit by the river and sulk, and then catch myself as I was working by the river, in nature! What an idiot.

My business was growing fast and my previous employer was now a fantastic client of mine.

Every six weeks or so I would either fly out to Calgary, or Nathan would fly back home. And each and every time Nathan would speak about how he wanted to come back, and that he had made a big mistake leaving me. Bless him. He was working 24/7 and he seemed so low. I told him he could come back anytime and I would of course support him in every way. It was his choice and I would be there for him no matter what. I even went out there to help him set it all up and get him mass national publicity.

I kept myself busy training for Ironman Canada during that time. It was a life goal of mine and what a great distraction.

Here's some excerpts from a blog I wrote during that time.

OCTOBER 21, 2014
JOIN ME FOR THE RIDE OF A LIFETIME

Name: Natalie Bruckner
Goal: Ironman Canada
Days until race: 9 months and counting
Miles cycled on Cascade Fluidpro Bike Trainer: 0
Miles cycled on Cascade CMXPro Power Exercise: 0

I've finally done it. I've signed up for my first Ironman Triathlon. With record numbers now signing up to compete in a race that consists of a 2.4-mile (3.86 km) swim, a 112-mile (180.25 km) bike ride and a marathon run of 26.2-mile (42.2 km), this is hardly groundbreaking news.

But let me introduce myself. My name is Natalie Bruckner, and just ten years ago you wouldn't catch me even running around the block. I hated it. Yet in a little over nine months I will be an Ironman competitor (and finisher hopefully).

Cycling and swimming have always been my forte, and having competed in a number of triathlons, including the Ironman 70.3 in Oliver, BC, Canada, I was ready to tackle Ironman Canada. Another one to tick off on my list of things to do before I'm 40. But living in "The Great White North" means training over the winter months can get a little difficult. I have no issues running in the rain in Vancouver, BC, (well we have no choice), and heading to the pool to do laps is actually pleasurable during the cold winter months, so my dilemma was, how was I going to build up the miles on my bike with slippery, wet and often snowy conditions during the months when training is meant to ramp up?

And so I started researching static bike trainers. I had heard some horror stories about stability and equipment failures, so I needed recommendations, and fast, and a fellow triathlete referred me to Cascade. After touching base with Anne at Cascade and chatting about my goals, it made sense to try the Cascade Fluidpro bike trainer as well as the Cascade CMXPro Power Exercise Bike.

Greedy, perhaps? But while the Fluidpro static bike trainer would allow me to increase my mileage while using my own bike (ensuring my setup was correct and to get the feeling of being on the road), the Fluidpro spin bike would help me to develop my cardiovascular strength and muscle power. And in truth, when you have an indoor training goal that consists of four to five hours a week on the bike to begin with that would soon be increased to around eight to ten hours a week leading up to the race, anything I could do to keep motivation up and vary my training was going to be highly beneficial.

When the "goodies" arrived at my house, I was like a child. I didn't want to wait for my husband (usually the DIY person in our house) to get home and help me assemble the equipment, so I ripped the packing apart and started reading the instructions. It looked far too simple....and as we all know from IKEA products, that's not always the case.

However, within 20 minutes I had both the Cascade Fluidpro and the Cascade CMXPro Power Exercise bike set up in my basement...I mean home gym. You see there were no missing screws, no extra tools required, it was all there for me with a step-by-step instruction guide.

Of course, any sensible person would have changed into their workout clothes and tested the bikes. Not me. I couldn't wait and hopped on in my work clothes and was like a child at Christmas. I was amazed at how stable the equipment was. The components are sturdy and the most exciting part is, I can track my miles, my heart rate, my cadence, speed, watts, time and distance with the wireless FLUIDPro Power meter.

I took countless images to send to my friends, proudly stating the "real" training was about to begin. Time for this Ironman to get on her bike.

MAY 11, 2015
Goal: Ironman Canada
Days until race: 4 months and counting
Miles cycled on Cascade Fluidpro Bike Trainer: 170 miles
Miles cycled on Cascade CMXPro Power Exercise Bike: 420 miles

April was an interesting month. Training was going really well. I started to listen to my body to figure out how much fuel I needed for the longer bike rides and runs, swimming was a blast and everything was going, well, swimmingly...and then, snap! Literally. I was out on what was going to be a two-hour run, on a glorious evening, a big smile on my face when I suddenly rolled my ankle and fell to the ground. A woman came rushing over to ask me if it was broken. I held back the tears as the pain shot through my foot and told her I didn't think so. Twenty minutes later I hobbled the two hour walk back up the mountain road home.

The bad news...

Two weeks later and I still wasn't able to put much weight on my left foot, so I decided to go to the doctor. It turns out I have a lateral malleolus *fracture (more commonly known as a stress fracture).*

It sounds bad, but, and here's the upside, the doctor told me he won't stop me from doing the Ironman, but that I should expect to be slow. I looked into deferring the Ironman, but unfortunately you have to compete in an event in the same year, and there's only one Ironman Canada. So here's the thing...either I give up my dream of competing in the Ironman this year and pay the $685 fee next year (yikes) OR I decide to suck up my pride and realize I will be slow and will probably end up walking the marathon part of the event.

The good news...

I have kept up training in the pool and my Cascade CMXPro Power Exercise bike has been a godsend. It has allowed me to continue training, but stop when my foot is feeling too fragile. Right now I am going to continue to train as best as I can with the goal of doing the Ironman in July.

It's not the best situation, but what a great conversation piece it will be if I complete the Ironman in under 17 hours and can say I did it with a broken ankle!

JULY 26, 2015
Goal: Ironman Canada. COMPLETED

I've done it. I am an Ironman!
Wow. Just wow. What a race. What a day.

It started off well with a fantastic swim. I had a moment of panic in the water, as I always do, but I pulled it together by repeating "you are in your own bubble." Then came the transition to the bike. It was so cold that my fingers stopped working and the volunteers came to the rescue, opening my bag and pulling out my essentials. Just as I climbed onto my bike the torrential rain came and it didn't let up until I hit Pemberton.

As I made the turn in Pemberton, the headwind meant I had to push myself harder on what would have been the easier part of the course, so I was thankful when I finally made it to the 30km hill climb that would lead me back to Whistler.

Then came the run. This was definitely more of a mental battle than a physical one. I knew with my fractured foot that I wouldn't be able to run the 42km, but in order to get to the finish line in time I would need to pull out the extra stops. On the second loop I could feel myself hitting the wall. With just 5km to go, my mind was overcoming some serious mental hurdles. One part of me was resigned to the fact that I just didn't have enough in me to carry on and the other part of me would not allow me to give up. It was at this point that I saw my husband Nathan and my best friend ZZ. They were there for me; to push me through what felt like a mental marathon. And as I crossed the finish line I was greeted by a sea of hands and cheers and those words from the announcer I had been hoping for all day: "Natalie Bruckner, you are an Ironman." I have never felt more alive.

I completed the course in 16:25: 48 with a MASSIVE smile on my face:
What made the Ironman such an amazing race for me however was something I hadn't considered before. The thousands of amazing volunteers and supporters who were there with us until the very end, that gentleman who greeted me at the finish line and ensured I didn't fall down, and most of all, my family and friends, my rocks. Without them I am certain this wouldn't have been possible.

Would I do it again? Had you asked me during the race I would have said no way. Today, let's just say I'm thinking about it!

Nathan has just under a year until he is home. He has already discussed it with his boss and is so excited. I am running my own business and, oh my gawd, life is so sweet.
At this point, I actually feel like I can conquer anything!

***

Chapter 39

A TALE OF TWO CITIES
(January 2017)

So, this was actually the original ending of the book. You know, the happily ever after.

When you read this, keep in mind that what's to come is very, very different.

Welcome back! I'm so glad you hung in there. I was just re-reading all my diatribe from earlier and I'm surprised you're still with me. I really do know how to go on, and boy was I negative. Poor me, woe is me, etc etc.

I can't figure out if I was just incredibly immature, or whether I am just a different person and Canada has taught me to chill out and be much softer and kinder (and more trusting); to appreciate the small things, and look at the good in people and in situations.

I think I've just grown up. Took me a while. But I keep thinking that and them, wham, another lesson or 50.

So, it has been almost 10 years since our move to Canada and what a joyride it has been.

Canada has been very good to us and is absolutely and utterly amazing. Actually, let me take that back. Vancouver and BC are utterly amazing.

The long distance thing with Nathan is working out great. Scary stuff.

Today, my business is thriving. I have the best clients and business partner.

My days consist of heading out for a lunchtime snowboard in Whistler, which is just 40 minutes up the road, hiking in the mountains with my doggie Fraggle and mountain biking on some of the world's best trails in between interviews, chatting with graphic designers and tending to clients needs.

That's in between being invited to dinner by the neighbours, friends, and people I only just met at the coffee shop. Squamish is quite the community.

As for Nathan, he is working hard in Calgary. It has been challenging for him setting up a dealership when oil prices in Alberta are so low, but he has done it, and done it well. Kudos to him. I am super proud of him.

And we have a date for him to return now. June 1, 2017. I cannot wait!

It hasn't been easy. Of course it hasn't. But it hasn't been as hard as I thought it would be. And every time I miss him, or feel sorry for me (silly girl), I walk along the stream and see the salmon run, or run into the mountains, or go snowboarding, or take advantage of the hot summer days we have here and swim in the lakes.

Yes indeed, we have amazing seasons. Shock, horror, Canada isn't blanketed in snow all year long. In fact this summer we actually hit 36.4 degrees Celsius. Does it rain? Yes it does. Oh yes it rains a lot. But rain in the winter means snow in the mountains.

It turns out Nathan's move was the best thing for us. It has strengthened our relationship. He says he feels a sense of fulfillment. It's like we have been given a second chance. When I look back at what I wrote, I can see the cracks were there. Maybe just a case of being together so long and the natural progression of some relationships. But being apart has made us learn about one another and, maybe more importantly, ourselves. I have learned a lot of independence. I managed to secure a mortgage by myself, find a property by myself for us, act as a landlord, grow my business, and get everything sorted, ready for Nathan's return. I have become a numbers girl as well as a wordsmith it seems. Business will do that to you.

I miss my family as much as I ever did, of course I do, but it comes in waves. And I am so lucky. Mum and dad just came to stay with me for a month (and they said they can't believe how happy everyone is here, including me), and my sister just came for a week. We all know we are here for one another and would hop on the plane in a second. The saying goodbye part never gets easier, still.

Nathan and his dad are getting on famously. He is actually in Valencia with his dad as I write this watching the supercar races. His dad is with his wife and they seem happy. It works. And they are great friends with my parents, which is wonderful. And I have to say, I adore Nathan's dad. We got to spend some quality time with each other recently in Calgary during the Calgary stampede, and we didn't stop laughing.

So here I am, 10 years older, finally applying for my citizenship (I know, I know, I should have done it sooner).

I once had a dream. To live in the mountains, experiencing a slower pace of life, with a dog.

And as I sit here and type, looking out at the snow on the mountains, with my snowboard bag packed ready for a weekend of snowboarding, my dog at my side, a successful business, and Nathan soon to be home, I can say that dream has more than come true for me.

Canada has been everything I dreamed of and more. It hasn't been easy and I have changed, but it has been an interesting challenge and I believe strengthened my character. Canada, is truly my home and where my heart is. While I can see it wouldn't be for everyone, I just love it here. For me, this is the best thing I could have ever done and I consider myself very lucky.

So, as I said, that was the original ending . . . you (and I) really had no idea what was to come.

***

Chapter 41

I WANT TO BREAK FREE
(January 2017)

Nathan is coming home for the weekend. I am so excited! It's only a few months until he returns and we can be together again.

His flight is a little delayed, so when he walks through the door looking, well, slightly angry, I kind of figure it's because he is tired. He has been super busy recently, and I'm sure the move is playing on his mind.

He greets our fluffy doggie and it's so sweet to see. Her little tail is going like a windmill on speed. But something is up. He isn't looking at me. So I go over and give him a hug. It's like hugging a stone. He must be tired I suppose. Our conversations have been great and super loving recently.

I tell him I painted the entire house, all the doors, baseboards, replaced the doors and handles. I feel so proud. His response? "Not now Nat, I have just walked in."

He must be tired. I grab him a beer, and we sit and chat about his day. He tells me he wants to check the house out in Lynn Valley tomorrow as we are selling it and he will be gone for a while. I think it's slightly odd he hasn't asked me to go, it's unlike him, but maybe because we want to put the house on the market soon it is playing on his mind.

We head to bed, and he turns away.

The next morning, he gets up early and races off to North Vancouver, so I do some work and go out with the doggie for a walk. When he comes back he tells me he wants to go snowboarding with his friend on Sunday, but because the daycare for dogs is closed at weekends, I won't be able to go. So I tell him I thought we were going to head out on Monday to Whistler to go snowboarding. He tells me he wants to spend time with friends too, which I understand, but he only saw his mate a few weeks earlier when he was out in Calgary and I haven't seen him in a month.

I am a bit put out by this to be honest and more because he seems quite angry for some reason. I notice he is taking his phone everywhere with him. That's pretty unusual. He normally ignores his phone when he is here and relaxes. I also notice his home screen has changed from the picture of us he has had on there for well, forever, to him and a car. Ah well, maybe he just wanted something different?

I head upstairs and when I come back down he is frantically texting. I peer over and ask if everything is OK? I see he has sent a number of messages in a row and when he sees me look he pulls his phone away. Heck, now I am suspicious. There is something off.

I ask him who he was texting so frantically to. Good lordy, I hate hearing myself this way, but something is definitely different. Something is up. I can feel it and now I am seeing it. He says his work colleague and brings up an entirely different text to the one I saw. OK, it's time to be a bit blunt, I really don't want to be mistrusting, but these signs are really not good. So I ask if I can look at his phone? He suddenly gets really angry. I can feel my blood start to boil. If he had always been protective like this over his phone I wouldn't think anything of it, but this is, well, so not him.

So I push again, very calmly I say, "Let me see who you were texting." He turns the other way and swipes left on a message. He has just deleted something. I can't believe it. What's he hiding? He hands over his phone and hovers over me before quickly grabbing it back.

Weird thing is, a few weeks before I had a dream he was heading out to lunch every day with a random girl, and I had told him about this dream in passing. The next day he told me he had been heading to the gym with some girl who worked at the local coffee shop, but there was nothing in it. My dreams can be weird sometimes and have come true, so should I be listening to them?

Then we begin the discussion again about snowboarding. I ask him if he wants to go with his mate on Sunday and I go with Zuzia on Monday (who I have to say has become an absolute rock in my life), and his face lights up. OMG, I know I shouldn't have asked that question, but I wasn't expecting that response.

He actually doesn't want to spend any time with me.

I tell him I am sad as I haven't seen him for a while, and he doesn't really respond. Is he stonewalling me again?

Now I feel paranoid.

This isn't me. I trust him so much and have always really respected his high morals, but suddenly I feel pushed out, excluded. I make him dinner, my homemade soup that has gone down so well with my neighbours, and he tells me it's a little bland. Le sigh.

I decide to make an effort and ask my neighbour if she will look after Fraggle if we go snowboarding the next day. She's so kind and agrees without hesitation, and so Nathan phones up his mate to arrange heading to Whistler.

We have a great day on the mountain, and Nathan seems OK. Not great, but OK. He tells his mate how excited he is to be coming home and coming home to me. I'm still wondering what's up however. When we get home he is really off and tells me he is just busy and can't think of anything right now. He starts complaining about BC and the only thing he wants to talk about is work.

He then tells me, he isn't sure if he still wants to be married and that his life now is in Calgary.

WTF? Where the. . . . where has this come from?

I am in shock. I can feel the tears well up in my eyes.

It is just a few months until he returns and he has been telling everyone, even his mate today on the slopes, that he is excited about moving back in June. Is he joking?

I am gobsmacked, and when I ask him about it, he again tells me he can't think right now and that he needs to get a car show out of the way before we can discuss it. He also tells me he doesn't think it's right for me to come out to Calgary in a few weeks for a friend's birthday as we had originally planned.

This is turning into a nightmare.

I can feel my world crumbling down around me. Is he saying what I think he is saying? He won't discuss it any further, and he heads out. And now, suddenly the date when he says his boss has said about moving back and other small things aren't quite adding up. Things I knew were off, but ignored.

Was I blind? And if so, what was I meant to be seeing?

I am in such a state. I decide that if he doesn't want to talk, I will write him an email (cue eye roll). But perhaps seeing it in writing he will realize his treatment is a little harsh, and how low down on the list of priorities our relationship seems right now. In the past he has been better with the written word than face to face open discussions.

I head out with Fraggle for a walk.

When I come back, he is stood there. He is acting normal. Then he says, "I read your email. The only reason I don't want you coming to the birthday is that the timing is wrong and it will cost us a lot." Seriously, of all the things I put in the email about not telling me the truth about what his boss had offered him as a job here, how awful this made me feel that our relationship wasn't a priority, how coming home angry and me getting excited to show him I painted the house ready for him and his annoyed reaction, nothing else struck a chord aside from not going to a birthday and me not heading out to Calgary?

He isn't willing to talk and I am in serious shock.

Then he tells me he has a meeting in Vancouver the next day and is flying out in the evening. Hang on a minute, he had told me his flight was in the morning. What's going on?

Honestly, I am too shocked to say anything, and hope he is just over-worked or panicking for some reason about the move. But, what if, what if he is seeing someone? That would explain the sudden change of heart about moving back and hiding his phone and not wanting to be physically close with me.

He goes out to clean my car.

While he is out there I am chatting with the neighbour and see Nathan suddenly walk into the garden and something is wrong. He has put his back out.

We get ice, heat and when I am sure he is OK, I head out to get some painkillers.

The next few days are all rather surreal. I am with this man, who has told me he isn't sure if he wants to be married anymore, and he is lying in bed, in pain, and he can't move. The following morning, he tries to get up and is in severe pain. So I phone up 811, which is HealthLink BC, and they talk me through what to do. We call an ambulance and the paramedics are here within five minutes and take him to hospital. I whip the dog round the neighbours and head on down. My neighbours rock.

In the hospital he asks me to delay his flight for a few days, so I ask if I can grab his e-ticket, which is on his phone. He refuses. He won't give me his phone and says I need to look it up another way. Even when he is in pain and on morphine, he still won't give me access to his phone?

I'm trying to put on a brave face, I really am. And I want to help him, but I have no idea what is happening right now.

Four hours later we head back home and for the next few days I care for him. If I'm honest, am I happy about it? Not particularly. I am caring for someone who has hinted that he no longer loves me.

What a situation.

A few days later he heads back to Calgary. No further discussion. He won't talk.

I'm in a state, What does this mean. Do I have to be kept "on hold" until he is less busy. What was the business with the phone? Is he depressed? Is he sick? So many unanswered questions. That night he tells me he is tired and can we give FaceTime a break for a bit. I give in...but I also need answers.

I can feel my blood pressure rising. I'm not sleeping. I am so confused. So I ask him if I can come and see him in Calgary that Thursday. He tells me he is too busy. I tell him I need to see him as I am in a real state since he dropped the bomb and I think it's essential to spend time together and for me to be a part of his life. He agrees that I can come and see him the following week and books a flight.

Hopefully I can sort out whatever the hell is going on.

It's February 2017 and I'm ready to get on a plane to Calgary.

I've got a stupid amount of work on right now, but our relationship comes first. So I arrive at the airport early so I can get work done.

Originally Nathan suggested we go to Banff hotsprings for a day. A good sign, right? So I want to be sure I am work free for the weekend and really be a part of his life because maybe it's the move, and maybe I need to rethink things. But now he says he is going to be really busy and might need to work. OK, I get it. He is busy, and it will give me a chance to be sure I don't fall behind with work too. The key is to be in his life for the weekend.

When I arrive in Calgary, he picks me up and looks pretty happy and suggests we go for a meal. Sounds good.

We are at Browns restaurant and I ask him how he is feeling. He tells me he loves Calgary, he doesn't plan to return to BC and resents me for not moving out to Calgary. I actually understand, I do, because I think that's a fairly natural reaction, but I tell him I could say the same and resent him for going, but that is in the past now and we had talked about this and how he always said, like every few days, how he wished he hadn't gone and couldn't wait to come back. How was I to know any different?

He tells me his life is his work and he doesn't see how our future can work out together. BAM. There it is. I feel those damned tears again and I don't want to sit in a restaurant crying, so I head outside for air. I want to leave. I want to go now. But it is -27 degrees here, and I have no clue where I am. I take some deep breaths, head back in and he is sat there. Zero expression. He is stone cold. We pay the bill and leave.

On the drive home the next blow is thrown. He tells me he has been feeling this way for six months now and knew he wasn't really coming back then. Six months? But we went on vacation to Arizona six months ago and had such a laugh. And then he came back at Christmas and told all our friends how excited he was to be coming back. He sent me flowers a few weeks earlier professing how much he missed me and couldn't wait to be with me again. Even his colleagues were talking to me about his return and how excited he was.

Did I miss the signs? Six months. The trauma of the past two weeks and this final blow is too much for me. I start crying, like really crying. I try to control my breath but begin to hyperventilate. I can't breathe. I just can't breathe. I go to open the car door to get some air and he grabs my arm. "Breathe Nat, breathe."

We head upstairs to his apartment and I am in tears. He just stands there. Nothing. Even a friend would reach out to another friend to comfort them after knowing them for 16 years wouldn't they?

We sit down and he starts answering my questions. He says he resents me for the fact his only friends are clients because if I was there, I would bring friends into our lives. He tells me he hasn't gone out to enjoy things because he feels bad that I may be put out, to which I tell him I am not the kind of girl that would ever stop him and I've never said anything like that. His response is that he is worried in case girls are around. I am shocked. Why would that matter? I tell him so. He says it does. He tells me he is envious of my life in Squamish, even though he knows he could have it.

And then, he tells me the one thing that explains so much. "I actually thought you would give in after a few months and come out to Calgary. You can be stubborn, but this time there was no leeway." WTF? He had been talking about moving back to B.C. since he first arrived in Calgary. How on earth was I to know? This was always meant to be temporary. He told me he had an agreement with his boss that it would just be for two years, and he told me that at the end of last year it was agreed that he would be back by June 1. How was I to know anything different?

And I am tired of running. Tired that every time we build a new life, he suggests moving, and up until now I had always followed. Leaving behind friends and family, because, it always seemed like an adventure. But now, I am starting to realize he is just running from something.

I tell him this. I tell him that for some reason, he runs from people who love him. He says, "I know, I know it's a problem. I know I do it."

Well, I suppose that's something. He is recognizing this. And it is likely I have been an enabler all this time by running with him. Until now. Until the Calgary situation came up. But to me, it made no sense. He wasn't going to be earning more money. In fact, we would be worse off. And not living in the mountains (yes, I know, I know, the mountains are only an hour or so away), but I mean living IN the mountains...you know, that simple life we always talked about. And with such an amazing group of friends too.

Had I gone to Calgary, well he works six days a week and very long hours, and when he's not working, he's on his phone. That's not the life I, and back then, we, envisaged when we moved to Canada.

I have to go for a cigarette, like now.

We are stood outside and I ask him, if I were to come out to Calgary for a few months, would that work. "It's too late," he responds. And so I ask him if he would go to relationship counselling. He tells me no, he doesn't believe in it. Every olive branch I am handing out is being ripped out of my hands and being crushed right into the ground. So what? This is it. This is the end?

So 16 years together and 12 years married and he is not even willing to give it one last kick of the can? There has to be someone else doesn't there? Or it's a mid life crisis? Or, oh my goodness, is he is depressed? He has all the signs. The dramatic weight loss, not sleeping, emotional shut down. I ask him. He laughs about the mid life crisis angle, and says, "maybe, it would make sense."

He then tells me I should fly out a day earlier as he is too busy right now, and to please leave him alone for a few days. No contact. He also asks that no-one in my family contact him, as he doesn't want things to get nasty and knows how protective they are of me.

OK. I'm not stupid. I know when I am not wanted, but I want to try, as long as it isn't an affair. But he has shut me down.

We go for something to eat at a local restaurant that I asked to go to, and he is acting weird, hanging his head as we go in. I ask him why, and he says nothing. Is there someone in here he doesn't want to see? Seriously. Is he, what, is he cheating on me? Because this behaviour all adds up to that. I try, I try and have a fairly normal conversation, even talk about fun times, but every time I catch him smile, it is like he quickly draws a curtain on it and hangs his head, like he doesn't want to remember, or be happy, or let someone see him happy.

When we get back to his apartment he tells me he needs to go for a drive. Crap. I'm paranoid. Is he going to apologize to someone for not being around? Or being in the restaurant with his wife? I see his ipad on the side. Before I know it, I open it. His history pops up, which has random things on it, including how much it costs to spend a season in

Breckenridge (what's he thinking? He wants to disappear? Or is he reminiscing?) and then his Facetime shows a call to a local number. That's not like him. He doesn't like FaceTime at the best of times, but it's rather random he would FaceTime someone local. Oh no. Is this a girl? I press call, but have a change of heart. Do I want to know? I mean really? Am I being foolish? What am I thinking? This is not me. I don't do this crap. What is happening to me?

He comes storming through the door a few minutes later. "Who did you call?" I tell him I wondered if he was having an affair. He tells me it is a client and that I better not interfere. I had jotted the number down in my phone, just in case. He told me he would be sleeping in the lounge tonight and he refuses to talk to me. I know I shouldn't have done that, but I am grasping at straws now. I just want to know the truth. That's all I want in a relationship. Trust and respect, and right now I am getting neither.

I fly back to Vancouver a day early and let Zuzia know as she is looking after Fraggle, and I get home utterly exhausted.

Poor Zuzia hears it all. The emotional diarrhea is unstoppable. I'm disappointed, shocked, upset, angry. I am grieving. In just a few weeks my entire life has turned upside down. The man I love doesn't resemble the man I knew and he is looking at me with almost hatred in his eyes. And although he says "it's all my fault Nat, it's all me," all I can think of is the one promise we made before he left for

Calgary. Whatever happens, our relationship will always come first.

It was just one small, but very important promise.

Zuzia is like a rock. She cries with me, she gets angry with me, she questions with me. Every emotion. How could I have been so lucky to have found such an amazing friend here in Canada, we've been through so much already together and being empaths, we take on each other's pain.

I know I am not alone here in Squamish. I have so many amazing friends here. And then there's my family who are like an absolute rock and would do anything for me. And my friends in the UK. I have so much support, such an army behind me, but I feel so, so very alone. My heart is broken, my best friend is gone.

I tell Zuzia about the FaceTime number and I decide to call it. It goes through to a voicemail. My gut knew, and now I know.

***

Chapter 42

THE TENANTS MOVE ON. AND SO DO WE (March 15, 2017)

It's the tenants final day at our house in Lynn Valley tomorrow and we will be doing the walkthrough. Nathan is flying in to do it with me. I haven't spoken with him for four days, as per his request, and I am going to pick him up from the Lonsdale bus terminal at 11am and he said we can have a coffee before.

That morning, I get a text: "I've booked a car for tomorrow, actually cheaper than the train and seabus. Plus I need to stop at work so it makes it easier. I'll meet you at the house just before 1pm?"

He honestly doesn't want to be anywhere near me right now. It's like I have done something wrong. But what?

I have the doggie booked in for a vet appointment at noon as she has a lump in her leg and I need it checked, so I will just get on with my day and face the music when I have to.

The vet thinks the lump is just a cyst but will send the sample off to the lab. So I drop the doggie off at daycare and head to the house.

I arrive before Nathan and start chatting with our lovely tenant. Two years of looking after the house has been challenging at times, but I managed it by myself!

Nathan walks through the door, hardly says hello and starts scanning the house. I walk around with the tenant and everything seems in order. The tenant can see something is up. It's pretty obvious. We say goodbye and Nathan is busying himself. I ask if we can talk.

I tell him my suspicions and that after the weekend and his treatment of me, plus sending me home early because he is too busy and then going for a meal that same night spending $200 on our credit card, well that's all pretty horrible really.

He says that yes, he has lived with this feeling for some time. I ask him if he thinks anything of our relationship and if the 16 years of friendship mean anything, and he actually has tears in his eyes. For the first time, he is actually showing emotion. And it breaks my heart. I go to give him a hug. He stops me.

He says that we need to get the house on the market, sell it, split the profits and just move on. He says its time to discuss the D word, yes, divorce. He tells me he will leave that with me to sort out.

Wait. What? I have to do it? But. He is the one who wants it. Why am I the one being left to sort it? I don't understand. Not one bit.

We say goodbye and as we do he hands me his accounts. Really? He still expects me to do the paperwork? I am stunned and I just take them. I stand there with them in my hands.

It's all business now.

What if he is depressed? I would never walk away from someone in that state of mind. So I send him a link to how emotions can be switched off in a relationship due to depression. I mean, he has had a tough time out there. He has worked his fingers to the bone, from trying to set up the dealership, staffing, and basically running the whole place.

I receive a text message the next morning:

Morning. I did read your email and thank you for thinking of me but I honestly don't feel depressed. I don't want you to hang on a glimmer of hope. Let's move things forward as we talked yesterday. I honestly think that's fairer and easier on both of us.

Glimmer of hope is gone. He's gone. Stop clutching at straws. I need to stop thinking it's me, or there's another reason. I know the reason. My heart is broken and I am utterly devastated. I love him so much.

Nathan asks me to meet up with the realtors. I do. Of course. I have been dealing with everything for the house for years, so it seems normal. It's just awkward timing as I have multiple deadlines. I receive a call from the vets as well. It seems the lump in the doggie's leg has some abnormal cells, so the vet wants to book her in to have that lump, and one on her tail removed. I can't imagine life without my dog. She's my trusty companion. I rescued her from an abusive background and we basically saved each other. It puts everything into perspective. Right now, my true loyal companion is the most important thing.

I go and meet the realtors, lovely guys, and we walk through the house, and discuss various options.

Awkwardly they know someone Nathan works with and they talk about him coming back in June. He even told his colleagues and the realtors he is still moving? I'm not good at lying, and so I just say he is busy and we don't know when he will return. I can't keep this up. I'm breaking inside knowing the truth and yet, I can't tell anyone as it's up to Nathan to tell his people.

The house valuation is just over a million. That doesn't excite me. Yes, I really do want to be able to afford to continue living where I live. To lose who I thought was my forever man, the man I would grow old with, plus my home, and having to find a place where I can have a dog in this market, well, let's face that bridge when I come to it.

I agree with the realtors that I will wash the deck clean, paint a couple of walls, fix a window and a few smaller things. Nathan said he would come back for a week to sort the house, but there is no need. I've had it covered for years, so why not just finish this off. I send him a message letting him know the details.

He sends me a frantic text. Obviously he is stressed as he feels out of the loop. So I phone him, and say he can ask me questions and anything I can't answer, the realtor can. He says, "Don't get excited about the price." Really? Did he really just say that? "I am far from excited about any of this believe me," I respond. I race home, work until midnight and then the next morning have to phone a lawyer.

The next few days I am busy sorting out the house, the lawyer, work, Fraggle, and I am utterly exhausted. Nathan is pushing me on things, and I finally snap. He has had six months to deal with this crap in his head and he is giving me a week to decide on things. That's not fair. We are not in the same phase right now. Things are moving too fast and I feel like I am drowning.

That night I sit on the sofa.

It would all be so much easier if it all just went away. My future is nothing like it resembled. I am causing suffering to anyone around me who I let see me like this. Nathan is being so business like about it all. He just wants me gone. Maybe it would be easier that way.

I'm really here? That frickin black dog is here again?

I see my doggie at my feet. I think of my parents, my sister, my friends. They have been amazing, as always. Pull yourself back together. I look up the name of counsellor in Squamish and send one an email who looks so lovely. I didn't think I would get here so quick. But now I know I need help early and nip this in the bud. And I will keep talking to family. I will keep talking this time.

This isn't going to stay in my head. I ask Nathan to stop rushing me and to leave me alone for a week. He says he understands, but just thought it would be better for both of us to get this done. No. Not for me. I need to stop thinking about him. Now I need to stop trying to find reasons, worrying about him, protecting him. The damage is happening to me, and he doesn't care, so I need to. I need to put my energy back into me. There is no me and him now. Just me.

I visit the counsellor for a 30 minute free session. I start crying as soon as I walk through the door. Dammit. She catches me trying to stop myself. "Don't stop it. The people who release their emotions are strong, because they face them. Those who hide them continue to run away from them." Those words ring so true.

During our chat she offers me no advice but opens my eyes to a few things. The most profound of which is my guilt for not going to Calgary and being at fault for all of this. I tell her a few friends at the beginning, when he announced he was moving, asked if I was choosing Squamish over Nathan, and that I told them it's not that simple. "A relationship is never about doing what's right for just one person; it's about a balance. Recognizing what it is that makes you happy and fulfills your needs and balancing it with the other person. You can't just live to make the other person happy. That is no longer a relationship," she says.

I never knew I was harboring this guilt. But it's true.

"And if it were that simple, he chose Calgary over you."

Perhaps the cracks started right there. Maybe even before? Our paths were heading in different directions back then for a reason.

Was I tempted to move to Calgary? Of course I was. I would have done anything for Nathan. But I was tired of running, and especially running for materialistic gain. And he always said he wanted to come back. For once I wanted Nathan to put my needs first, and maybe, that was where the change came.

I realized I wanted to be number one for once. And I wasn't. Perhaps I never was . . .

***

Chapter 43

ANNIVERSARY DREAD

It's April 4, 2017 . . . exactly 12 years since Nathan and I got married. I knew this day would be tough and I wake up feeling so sick.

My friend Zuzia has come to stay, and I am thankful for that, but right now I can't face the world. I am finding it hard to face anyone. I don't have the energy. Not yet.

It just makes no sense that 12 years ago I was standing on the beach saying "til death do us part" and here I am, the man of my dreams, my best friend, isn't dead, but a part of him is. I just don't recognize who he is anymore.

He won't speak to me about anything aside from the sale of the house, or the separation agreement, and even then I am lucky if I get a response.

I have questioned every question there is, I suppose just looking for an answer, when there is no real answer that would help...but I am coming to the terms with the fact that this is who he is now. But after all this time to just throw me away like an old rag, I don't get it.

I roll over in bed and decide to write him a note. Afterall, the past 12 years, while we have had the usual ups and downs of any relationship, there have been plenty of good times, and I want him to know I appreciate that. No, I take that back, I just need to do this for me.

And so I send him an email:
Hi, I don't expect a response to this, I just wanted to wish you a happy anniversary. Despite us now taking a new road, I look back on the past 12 years with much fondness and celebrate the amazing times we had.
12 years ago today I stood on a beach and married my best friend. I will always treasure that and the adventures we had, the love we shared, the crazy amount of monkeying around we did and the copious amounts of laughter we had. Thank you for joining me on that journey and for being there with me to create many wonderful memories.
Nat

And so I stand in the shower for about 30 minutes, trying to wash the thoughts from my head before facing Zuzia, and then just burst into tears. Crap.

Thankfully I have quite a busy day with work to keep me busy and Zuzia says she wants to take me out for a meal in the evening. She really is an absolute angel.

I chat with mum and dad, who are obviously worried about me, and are themselves celebrating 49 years of marriage. I can tell they feel bad, but for me, to see such a wonderful couple that has worked through their own challenges and show such respect and love is truly inspiring. It shows me what really exists out there, and that's a beautiful thing.

Zuzia and I head for a coffee at lunch and sit in the sun, and then swing by some friends' houses. Life really is pretty sweet in Squamish. Such an amazing community.

That evening we head to the bar and grab some beers, wings and nachos. At one point I thought about ordering a cocktail, just because Nathan used to go on at me about how he thinks I should order cocktails instead of beer sometimes, because, well, it's ladylike. Hmmm, cracks....

We have a really lovely evening, and I begin to realize that this is actually the nicest anniversary I have had in quite a few years. Last year Nathan and I weren't together, and the year before that was when he went. I then get a text from my mate Dan in Australia, I say a text, it was a fabulous joke: Two flies are playing football in a saucer. One says to the other, "Make an effort, we're playing in the cup tomorrow."

This starts a stream of messages and puns, our speciality.

Zuzia and I head home to watch The Voice. It's just so relaxing being in her company, and I appreciate the good people I have in my life. This is my new

April 4. I will appreciate the good and let go of what was.

Of course I hear nothing back from Nathan, it's expected and I didn't want to. It was my way of saying goodbye and all the best. Kids these days call it closure I suppose.

***

Chapter 44

TIME TO REBUILD

The house has been on the market for one week and the realtors are getting stressed, as is Nathan, that it is overpriced. I remind them all it has only been one week. Seriously, it's a sign that people have got far too complacent in this hot market and now think if a house isn't sold within a few days something is up. I remind them all that we need time and the little rancher appeals to a select market. They all seem to calm down a little.

Nathan is constantly emailing me to sort out the separation agreement. I don't quite understand the rush, I really don't. I mean, perhaps he has to have a reason for it. It's not like I'm vindictive. I am realistic and realize things and people change, so I would just walk away. Maybe he just wants to quickly shut that chapter of the book.

I phone a few lawyers to set up appointments. My mum, the angel, is actually giving me a swift kick up the backside to be sure I get legal advice as she knows I am a soft touch. She has a point. I mean I worked my butt off since I have been with Nathan, and always been the one to bring in a steady wage. Plus, when he has been out of work, I have been earning, so it's fair I get what is rightfully mine. I don't want any more than that. My mum is speaking sense, and I know it, and right now I'm in an emotional well and I understand I won't be seeing clearly.

Talking of mum and dad, I've been skyping with them and my sister every day, and they truly are my rocks. They bring a certain balance to the table. My sister is like me, and understands where I am coming from and we laugh, dryly. My mum is the protector, so she is super angry and very financially focussed. And my dad is the soother. He remains quiet when you need it and then bursts out, which is so sweet. Of course he gets angry, and his occasional blowouts have actually made me laugh because it is so out of character, but he is definitely a leveller and provides my mum with a balance too.

And then there are my friends. Oh my gawd, what can I say about them. I knew I had amazing friends both in Canada and the UK, but they are basically all holding me up right now. I feel like I have an army of support behind me. In fact, I am so busy on text, meeting up with people, on the phone, that I hardly have time to sit and soak it all in.

My sister has been an angel, and told friends to give me room to breathe, which makes so much sense. Sometimes, being around people all the time during moments like this can be overwhelming and I definitely need my space. But how do you tell friends who are trying to be supportive that you just need to be alone for a bit? But I get it. And I truly appreciate it as well. What would I do without them?

Every day is a roller coaster of emotions ranging from WTF to this is good. Move on.

Heck, what a ride.

Two weeks after the Lynn Valley house is on the market and we get an offer. It's time to play the property game. And so we counter. And they counter. And we counter. And they counter. And then Nathan calls me. "What would it take for you to sell?" This surprises me. He was always the money guy, but here he is asking me? OK. "What if I give you the extra and so we just get this done?" WHAT? Who are you? What have you done with Nathan? Oh wait, silly me! He disappeared back in January. I agree to his terms. The house is sold and exchange will happen on June 6, 2017. It gives me just enough to be able to take on my home in Squamish . . . just about.

It's time to prepare the house. Fix some things and get it finally ready. It's a chance for me to truly cleanse in every which way. And I've been caring for the house for the past two years, it is kind of second nature to me now. I pop down to the house and bump into my neighbours. I inform them what is happening, giving them loose details, and they are shocked. Tell me about it!

As I sit on the deck after completing most of the chores, I pull out a cigarette. Inhale. Exhale. I know

I shouldn't be smoking, but right now, I have to give myself a bit of a break. A chance to feel like I too am being naughty.

Jeez. Honestly. How did it come to this?

Since it has happened, I've had numerous conversations and didn't realize quite how common this is. It seems some guys just hit 40 and WHAM. They want a life change.

I have to say, it was a good 16 years and I have no regrets. But what a shocker.

Oh life, you really are interesting.

(May 31, 2017)

It has been about six months now since Nathan dropped the original bomb and how do I feel? I'm OK.

I understand that unlike most marriages that end in divorce, I had a head start when Nathan moved to Calgary. And when I think about it logically, that's when the actual separation happened – in fact it really happened when he chose Calgary and I didn't.

I had to learn to be on my own, to rediscover what I love to do, to gain independence, to eat what I want to eat and to be alone. I mean honestly, we saw each other for a maximum of five weeks a year. Who was I kidding when I thought everything was fine!

You can see me rolling my eyes at myself, can't you? What a goon.

My day to day life is unchanged. Actually, that's not quite accurate. My day to day life is about more independence and doing exactly what I want to do. I get to work the hours I want, head out into nature, go biking/snowboarding/running without thinking I should be working harder to get more and more and more money. I work hard so I can cover me and my expenses. Or be home in time in case I get a call. I realize, it's the first time I have been truly selfish.

As per Nathan's wishes, I sort the separation agreement and that was finally signed last week. I am in the process of transferring the mortgage in Squamish into my name as my wage is enough that I can keep the house and we are just tying up the loose ends.

I went back down to the Lynn Valley house the other day in fact and the grass is overgrown and a part of the roof has come off. I try to reach Nathan to ask him if he thinks we should sort that ahead of the sale. He doesn't answer. The usual these days. When he came back a few months ago to pick up his stuff I truly let rip because he refused to talk, and he responded "you just need to move on Nat." He was right.

So, it is left up to me to sort the house out, and it makes me proud.

The paperwork involved in all of this is rather crazy, especially when you end up doing it yourself, but, when you hear about divorces, it always sounds like a legal nightmare. My experience hasn't been anything like that. Good lawyer I suppose.

Yes it helps we both wanted to keep it out of the courts and to limit lawyers fees, and that we've been fairly amicable about it. It's also good that it has been 50/50 pretty much all the time when it came to finances. My sister's sweetest comment that was echoed by a few people is that I have handled the whole thing with "dignity and grace." Possibly the biggest compliment I have ever received. What they haven't heard is my inner voice raging! Haha.

But seriously, as time has gone on, I don't miss him as much as I thought I would.

It definitely helps that he handled the whole situation badly by not communicating, but then again, had he sat me down and chatted, I may have been left sad at losing such a wonderful man. As it is, I am glad he went about it the way he did as it has made it easier to transition to the point of realizing he is not the man for me.

I also now see various cracks. You probably see them reading this too. It's just we got on so well as mates in general, it was easy to put a bandaid over those very cracks. I'm a people pleaser, and me standing my ground on not moving must have been a real big shock to him. It was out of character for me. And now I realize I am no longer that person. We have both grown, and changed.

We now know what happened and my hunch, well hunches often prove to be right. It's a mute point now. It happened. End of story.

My head is pretty clear. In the end we became two different people, and we were no longer right for each other. Our dreams were no longer aligned.

So now what?

I am finalizing all the paperwork and come mid June I will have my own house in the mountains, be swimming in the lakes, hiking with my dog and looking forward to the following snowboarding season. Oh and yes, I am a Canadian citizen now, with a Canadian passport too!

Who knew that my Canadian dream would come true? Just not exactly as planned.

I'm not going to lie, it's a healing process, but why lament a past that cannot be changed, when you have a future you can focus on and take control of? Oh, and did I mention I met a Canadian chap, a bush man, as he calls himself, who enjoys the simple things in life?

After all that crap that went on, the last thing I wanted, ever again, was a relationship. Isn't it funny how that happens? Life had other plans. He came walking into my life and my doggie adored him. That tells me something. He is a breath of fresh air. He points out the beautiful colours of a rainy sky, and laughs, and laughs, and laughs. He is full of love for the world, and the simple things.

I think Richard De Meath may be right; I feel richer today than I have ever felt right now.

***

Chapter 45

IN SUMMARY: WHERE THERE'S A WILL...
It's funny looking back.

The best way I can describe 2017 is this: one minute
I felt like I was sat all toasty, warm, and contented
in my home that I had built for many, many years
and the next, the person I least expected, came
along driving the biggest bulldozer and without
warning, the walls, roof, windows, everything came
crashing down on top of me.

I couldn't breathe. I was in shock. Why had
everything gone so dark all of a sudden? Why had
this happened? Where was I? I had so many
questions.

It felt like I lay there forever unable to move...and
yet, within minutes I heard something. Scratching.
Scrabbling. I could hear familiar and comforting
voices.

What I couldn't see was an army of people who had
dropped everything to come and rescue me. At the
front of the line, my family, and of course my soul
sister, lifting the heaviest bricks and breaking their
backs in the process to get to me. Behind them,
extended friends and family from near and far
gathered in their droves, using their tools to pull me
out from beneath the rubble. It was overwhelming.
It was amazing. Faces I had seen just a few days
earlier, and faces I hadn't seen for years were
reaching out to help.

Yes, I was cut, battered, and bruised, and the injuries would take time to heal and some would leave scars, but they would be proof of what I had endured.

As I began to reflect, I could see that my home had cracks. Multiple cracks. Yes, it wasn't perfect. But I had loved it with all my heart and I would have done anything to fix it.

And maybe I was wrong.

And so those very same family and friends stood with me as we began to rebuild my home on the same strong foundations, but in a new style that sometimes replicated my former home, and other times took a new direction with larger windows to allow more light to shine in.

Strangers suddenly appeared to help build this new home, and when the work got tough, one particular stranger came along to stand by my side and work 24/7 to ensure I would have a safe and secure home.

As I stand here now, looking at the brand new home that you so many helped me build (yes, you know who your are and many of your have suffered injuries yourself as a result of pulling me out), I can't quite find the words to say how thankful I am for the support.

How much those visits, those daily messages, those phonecalls, those cards...all those small things that you may not even realise, helped pull me through. You never quite know the impact you have on someone's life, but I can assure you that you have a greater impact than you will ever realize.

2017 was a challenging year, but one with so many plots twists and turns that it kept me on my toes and showed me that you just never know what life has in store, so yes, take time to mourn what was, but don't let it shadow what can and will be.

People make their choices for a reason, not everyone will understand why you chose your path, and that's OK, and questioning or trying to understand will not always help. And not everyone is meant to be in our lives forever. No regrets. Someday everything will make sense. And always remember that you are in fact enough.

This tale of my Canada journey, is, as I see it, far from over.

END

Printed by Amazon Italia Logistica S.r.l.
Torrazza Piemonte (TO), Italy